Stockton Bight
and sand dunes

Newcastle

Newcastle Airport

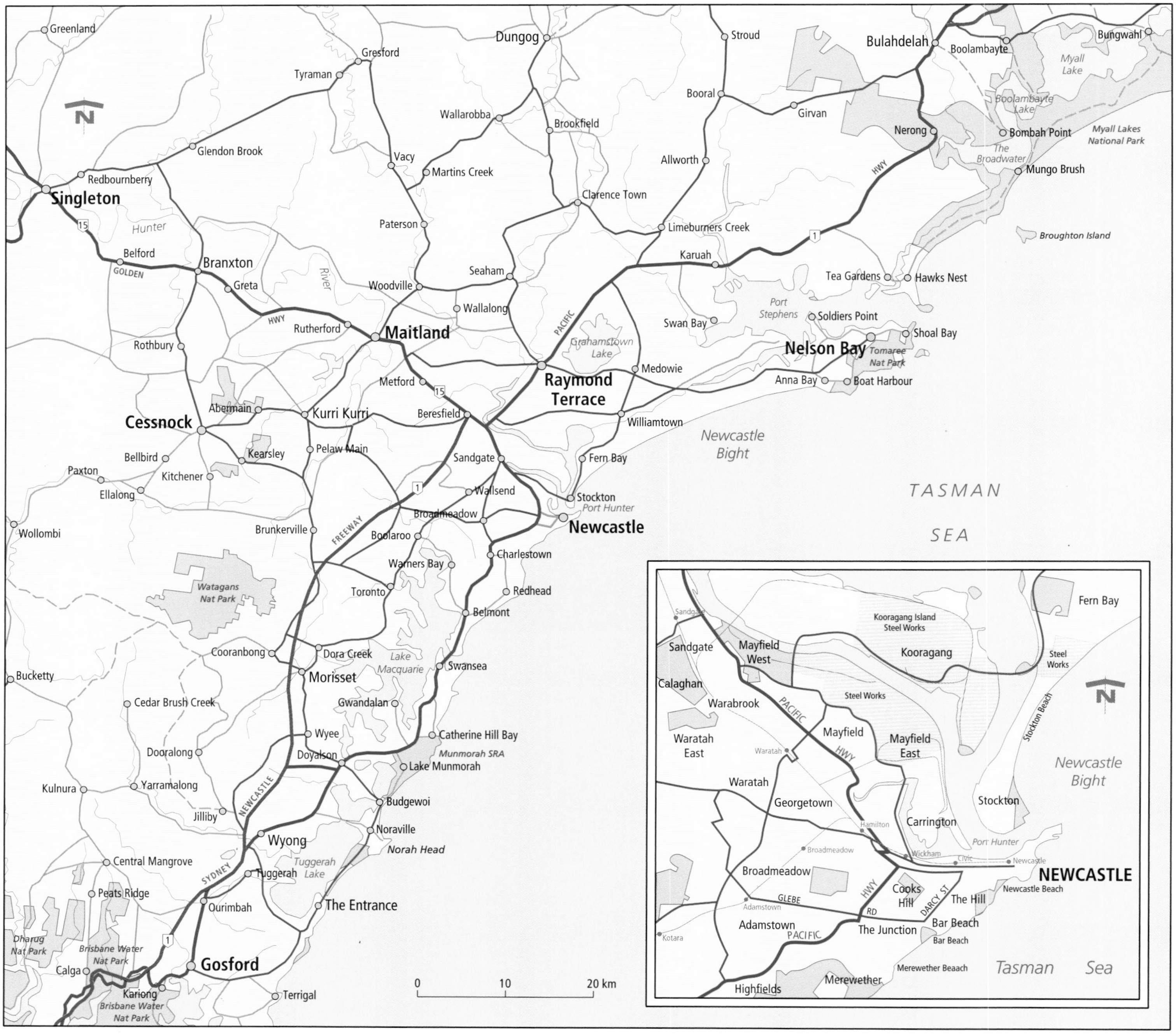
Greenland
Gresford
Tyraman
Dungog
Stroud
Bulahdelah
Boolambayte
Bungwahl
Myall Lake
Booral
Girvan
Wallarobba
Brookfield
Boolambayte Lake
Nerong
Bombah Point
Myall Lakes National Park
The Broadwater
Glendon Brook
Vacy
Martins Creek
Allworth
Mungo Brush
Redbournberry
Singleton
Clarence Town
HWY
Hunter
Paterson
Limeburners Creek
Broughton Island
15
1
Belford
Branxton
Karuah
GOLDEN
Greta
River
Seaham
Tea Gardens
Hawks Nest
Woodville
Wallalong
Port Stephens
Soldiers Point
HWY
PACIFIC
Swan Bay
Rutherford
Maitland
Grahamstown Lake
Shoal Bay
Rothbury
Nelson Bay
Tomaree Nat Park
Metford
Raymond Terrace
Medowie
Anna Bay
Boat Harbour
15
Abermain
Kurri Kurri
Beresfield
Terrace
Williamtown
Cessnock
Newcastle Bight
Bellbird
Kearsley
Pelaw Main
Sandgate
Fern Bay
Paxton
Kitchener
1
Ellalong
Wallsend
Stockton
TASMAN
Broadmeadow
Port Hunter
Newcastle
Wollombi
Brunkerville
FREEWAY
Boolaroo
SEA
Charlestown
Warners Bay
Watagans Nat Park
Toronto
Redhead
Belmont
Cooranbong
Dora Creek
Lake Macquarie
Bucketty
Morisset
Swansea
Cedar Brush Creek
Gwandalan
Wyee
Catherine Hill Bay
Dooralong
Doyalson
Munmorah SRA
Lake Munmorah
Kulnura
Yarramalong
NEWCASTLE
Budgewoi
Jilliby
Noraville
Wyong
Norah Head
Central Mangrove
SYDNEY
Tuggerah
Tuggerah Lake
Peats Ridge
Ourimbah
The Entrance
Dharug Nat Park
1
Brisbane Water Nat Park
Calga
Gosford
0
10
20 km
Kariong
Brisbane Water Nat Park
Terrigal
Fern Bay
Sandgate
Kooragang Island Steel Works
Sandgate
Mayfield West
Kooragang
Steel Works
Calaghan
Steel Works
Warabrook
PACIFIC
Stockton Beach
Mayfield
Waratah East
Mayfield East
Waratah
HWY
Newcastle Bight
Waratah
Georgetown
Stockton
Hamilton
Carrington
Port Hunter
Broadmeadow
Wickham
Civic
Newcastle
Broadmeadow
NEWCASTLE
HWY
Cooks Hill
Newcastle Beach
GLEBE
The Hill
Adamstown
RD
DARCY ST
Adamstown
The Junction
Bar Beach
PACIFIC
Kotara
Bar Beach
Merewether Beach
Tasman
Sea
Merewether
Highfields

newcastle

new century, new horizons

Ian Kirkwood and Christopher Ford

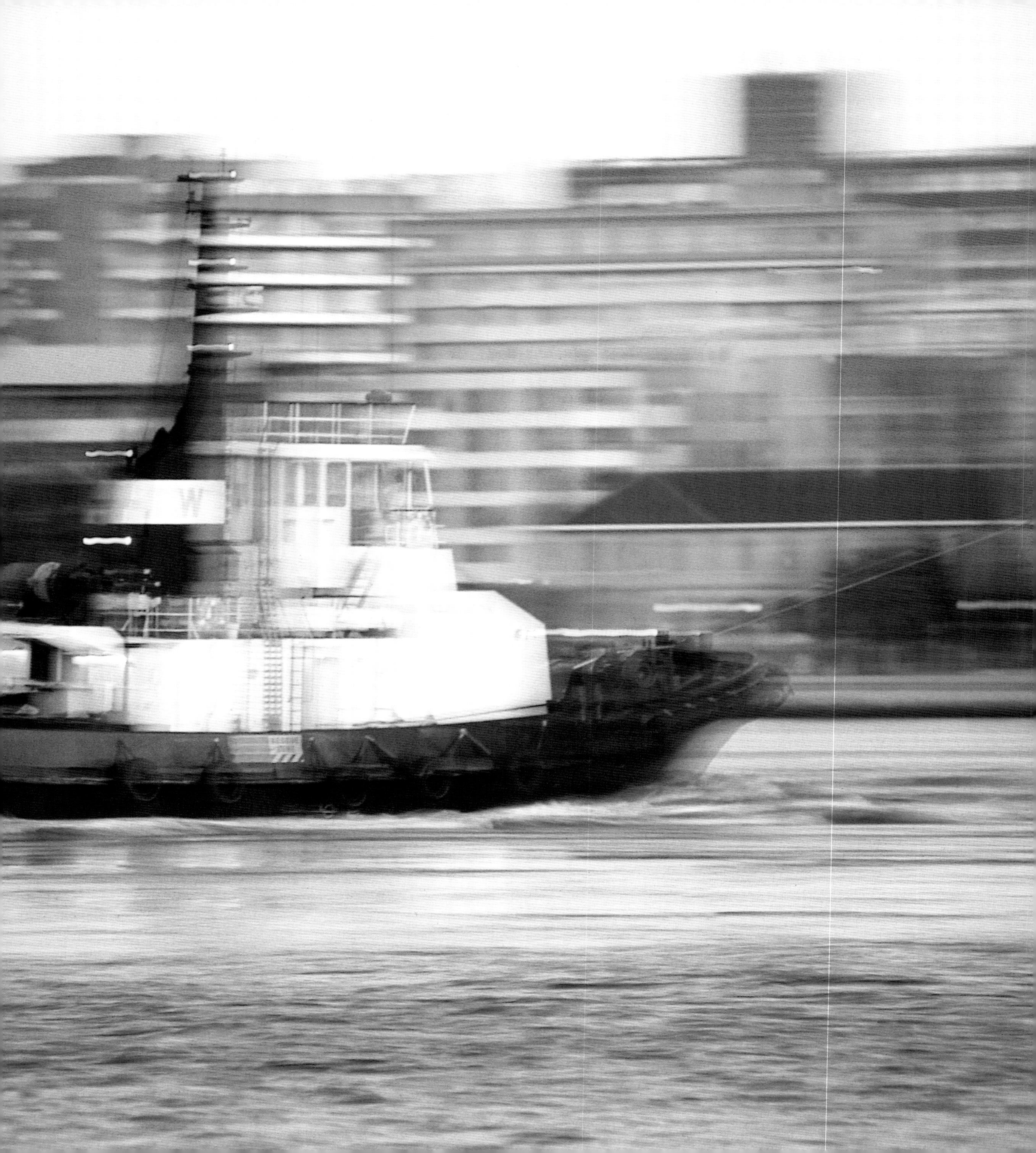

contents

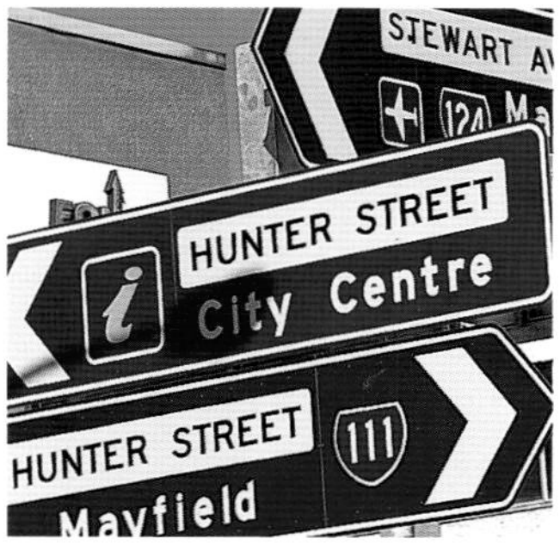
STEWART
HUNTER STREET
City Centre
HUNTER STREET
111
Mayfield

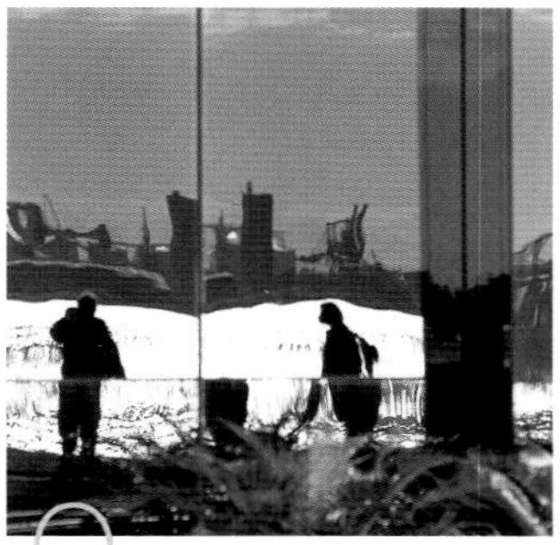

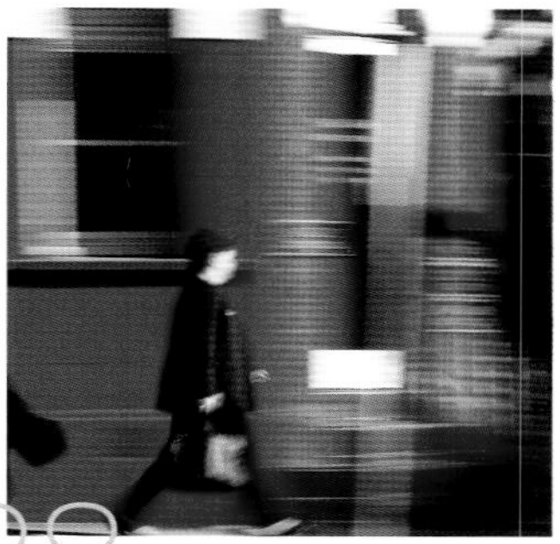

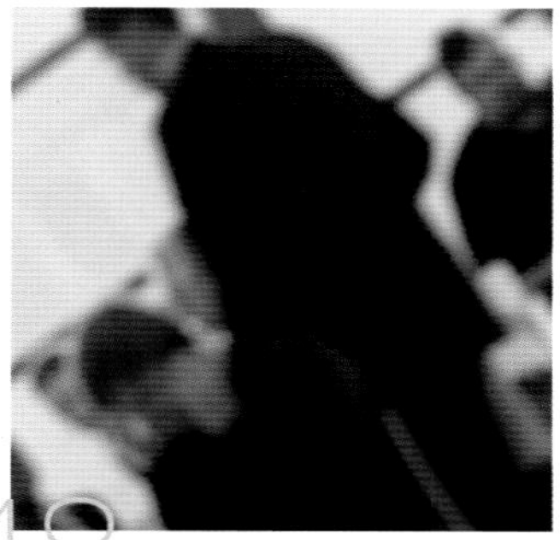

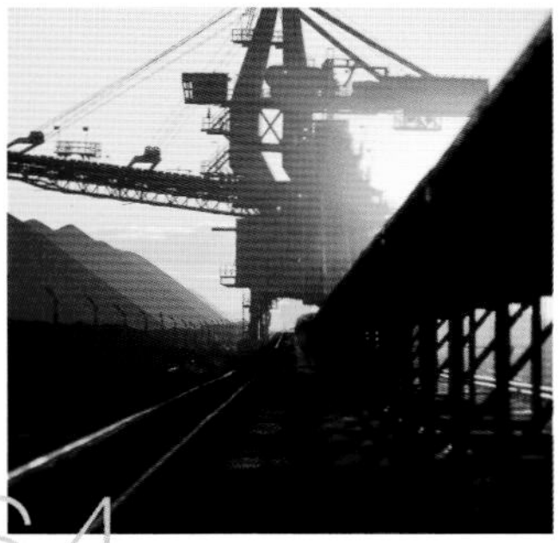

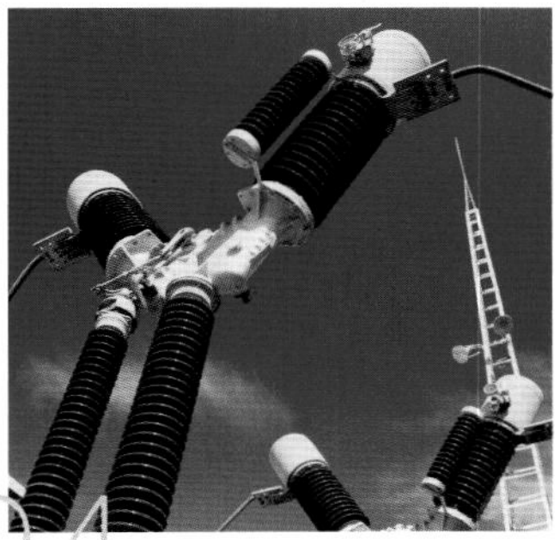

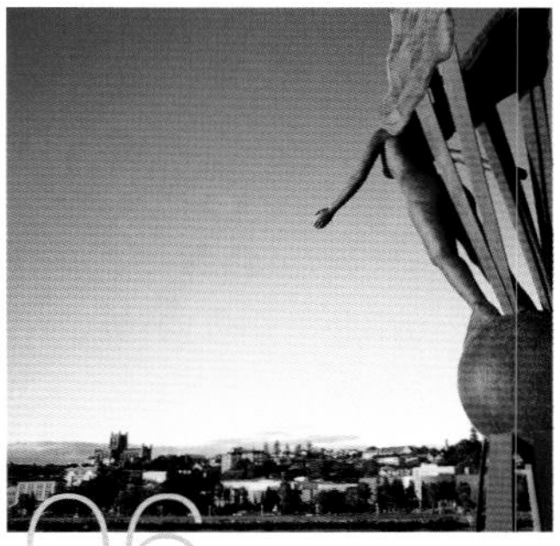

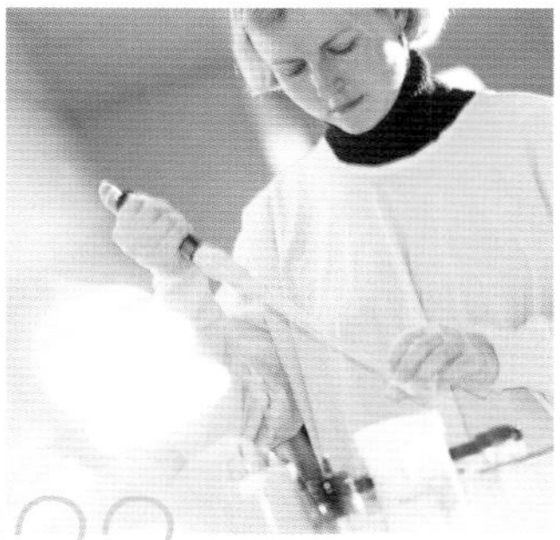

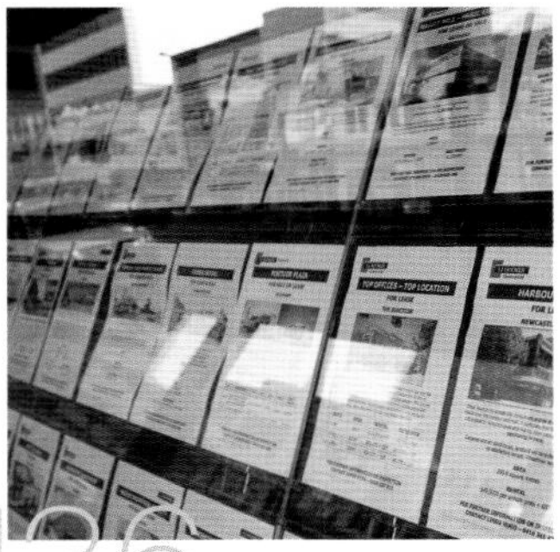

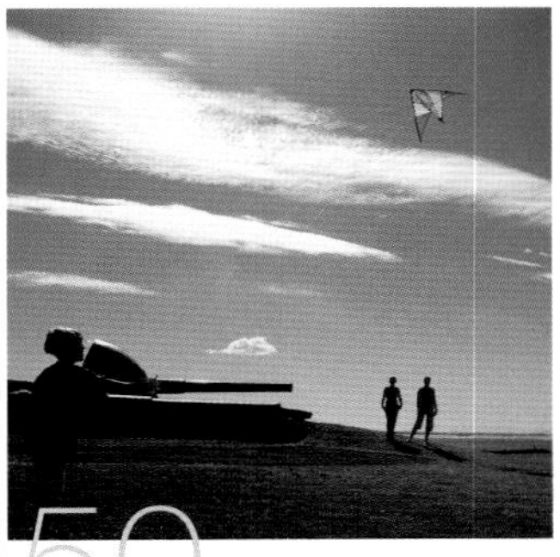

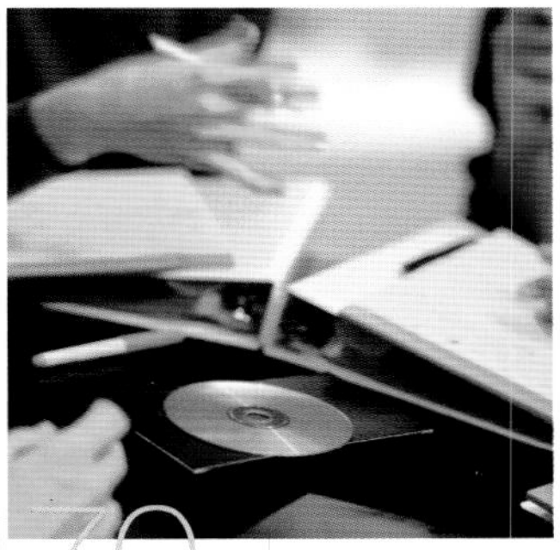

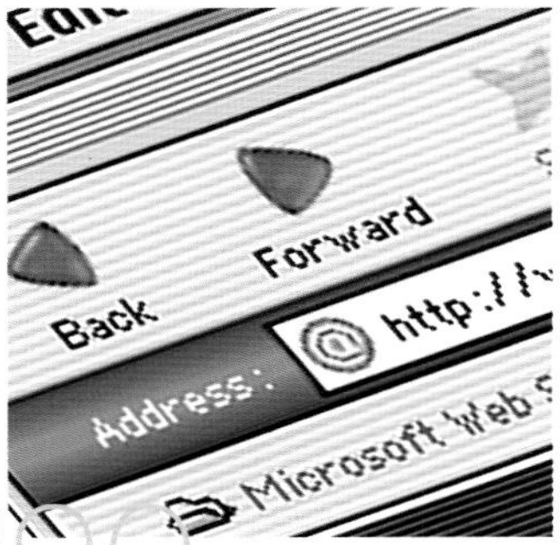
Back
Forward
Address:
http://

advisory group

Patron
Councillor John S Tate
Lord Mayor
The City of Newcastle

Chairman
Paul Anicich
Senior Partner
Sparke Helmore Solicitors

Advisory Group

David Brewer
General Manager
Port Waratah Coal Services
Limited

Paul A Broad
Managing Director
EnergyAustralia

Ric Charlton AM
Chancellor
The University of Newcastle

Ken Clifford
Chief Executive Officer
Hunter Region Academy
of Sport

Professor Robert Constable
Dean and Director, Faculty
and Conservatorium of Music
The University of Newcastle

Angus Dawson
General Manager
Honeysuckle Development
Corporation

Janet Dore
General Manager
The City of Newcastle

Glenn Evans
Chief Executive Officer
Hunter Catchment
Management Trust

Howard Frith
Managing Director
Newcastle Permanent
Building Society Limited

Gavin Fry
Director
Newcastle Regional Museum

Gaye Hart AM
Director
Hunter Institute of Technology
—TAFE NSW

Geoffrey J Leonard
Chairman
Hunter Medical Research
Institute

Professor Katherine McGrath
Chief Executive Officer
Hunter Health

Brian McGuigan AM
Managing Director
McGuigan Wines Limited

Dr Ken Moss
Chairman
Boral Limited

Dr Glen Oakley
CEO and Managing Director
Newcastle Port Corporation

Steven Rich AM
Chairman
Focus Publishing Pty Ltd

Colin Rogers
Chief Executive Officer
NIB Health Funds Pty Ltd

Gillian Summers
Executive Officer
Hunter Economic
Development Corporation

Sandy White
Manager *(Jan 1997–July 2001)*
Newcastle Airport Ltd

participants' roll of honour

inaugural lead participant

The City of Newcastle

major participants

EnergyAustralia
Marathon Tyres
Newcastle Airport Ltd
Newcastle Health Services
   Hunter Health
   Hunter Urban Division of General
   Practice
   Hunter Medical Research Institute
Newcastle Permanent Building Society
   Limited
Newcastle Port Corporation
Paul Foley's Lightmoods Pty Ltd
Robtec Control Solutions Pty Ltd /
   Control Synergy Pty Ltd
Sandvik Australia Pty Ltd
Varley Holdings Pty Ltd
Websters Australia Pty Ltd

key participants

ADI Limited
AOK Health Pty Ltd
Daracon Engineering Pty Ltd
Delta EMD Australia Pty Ltd
GrainCorp Operations Ltd
Honeysuckle
Horizons Golf Resort
Hunter Institute of Technology—TAFE
   NSW / The University of Newcastle,
   Australia
Ipera Network Computing Pty Ltd
Koppers Coal Tar Products Pty Ltd
Newcastle Newspapers Pty Ltd
NIB Health Funds Ltd
OneSteel Limited
Port Waratah Coal Services Limited
PW Saddington Pty Ltd
Sharp Electronics Office National
Sparke Helmore Solicitors
Stratchleys Restaurant
Toll Logistics
Tomago Aluminium Company Pty Ltd
United Goninan Pty Ltd
W Stronach Pty Ltd

foreword

Newcastle is one of the most exciting and dynamic cities in Australia. From a proud tradition as a national centre for heavy industry, the widely and affectionately known 'Steel City' has grown into a vital business, educational and cultural centre.

Newcastle has a lifestyle that is second to none. There are many that bear testament to this with home ownership rates better than the national average. Newcastle boasts Australia's lowest cost of living based on food and grocery indexes, and has world-class health and medical services, an internationally renowned university and quality education across all levels. We have a vibrant cultural community with theatre, music, food, wine and more. Our wonderfully clean beaches make way for some of the world's most well-known wine country. An interesting fact is that Novocastrians enjoy three times the national average of open space per person.

The advantages of a city environment in a regional setting flow onto Newcastle's commercial scene across all areas of business, and can be most readily explained as the result of marrying a regional cost structure with urban convenience. This means that the average cost of setting up a business in Newcastle is more attractive than in many capital cities, yet there are still the conveniences of transportation, technology and a commercial infrastructure that encourages competitiveness. Moreover, Newcastle is a comfortable 90-minute drive from Sydney.

Newcastle, New Century, New Horizons reflects the vast opportunities afforded by Newcastle's competitive commercial environment and lifestyle advantages. I encourage this publication as a comprehensive showcase of the city of Newcastle and the unique and triumphant Novocastrian spirit.

Councillor John S Tate
Lord Mayor, The City of Newcastle
Project Patron

introduction

Newcastle, New Century, New Horizons captures the essence of our progressive and industrious city. As Australia's sixth largest city, a highly competitive centre for commerce and the gateway to the vital Hunter region, Newcastle is a distinctive part of Australia.

An important aspect of Newcastle has been its transition from an economy largely based on traditional industries such as steel and coal, to one which is more diversely spread to include what are commonly termed 'new' industries. Some of these new industries are in manufacturing, while others are more service, process or research and development oriented.

One of the central driving factors in the minds of Novocastrians is the importance of continual change and constant improvement—a progressive attitude borne out of the distinctive Novocastrian spirit and the challenges, both industrial and natural, the people of Newcastle have faced. Newcastle's ability to 're-invent' itself has unsurfaced an entrepreneurial quality within the Newcastle community that offers boundless opportunities for enterprising companies.

Newcastle, New Century, New Horizons is a balanced and informative profile of Newcastle that presents the combination of strengths across all key business sectors   and the irresistible commercial benefits of setting up business in Newcastle. It is also a showcase of Newcastle's unbeatable lifestyle, education and training opportunities, and tourism and cultural highlights. This all makes *Newcastle, New Century, New Horizons* a valuable resource for anyone who wants to do business or invest in Newcastle.

Paul Anicich
Senior Partner, Sparke Helmore Solicitors
Chairman, Advisory Group

one

NEWCASTLE

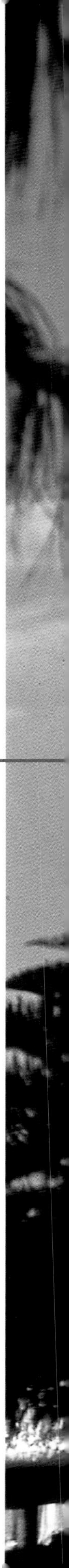

Newcastle is a booming

regional capital with a fantastic climate,
beautiful surroundings and a population
that enjoys a relaxing, coastal lifestyle.

Everywhere you look in Newcastle, change is afoot. The once industrial waterfront alongside the city's central business district (CBD) is midway through a 20-year transformation that will turn The Foreshore and Honeysuckle, the two adjoining development projects, into a maritime pleasure precinct equal to any.

Throughout the CBD, new apartment blocks and refurbished buildings are luring families back into the heart of the city. While the retail dollar has shifted to the booming suburban shopping centres, the Newcastle CBD is fighting back with the support of the Newcastle City Council and New South Wales (NSW) government planners.

'The earthquake was a big turning point in [Newcastle's] history. There were a lot of people who came into the region after the quake; coming here for work, initially only for a short time and they found a quality of life here. They found their kids could go to university and do a whole lot of things that [Novocastrians] have known about for years. We have so many good things going for us ... one of Newcastle's great assets is quality of life.'

—The Hon Richard Face, Minister Assisting the Premier on the Hunter

Popular finance magazine *Australian Business Monthly* stunned Australians when it announced that Newcastle was the nation's best city in February 1992. The magazine polled people in 24 Australian cities on 17 criteria from employment, housing prices and wages through to hospitals, schools and lifestyle, and when the results were tallied, Newcastle was at the top of the list.

The choice of Newcastle surprised many commentators, who dismissed the poll as an aberration—Maitland and Lake Macquarie ranked third and eleventh respectively. But a closer look at the city showed the rest of Australia what Newcastle residents, Novocastrians, already knew: there is much more to Newcastle than steel and heavy industry.

Newcastle is a booming regional capital, with a fantastic climate, beautiful surroundings and a population that enjoys a relaxing, coastal lifestyle.

It's no accident that Newcastle, Australia's sixth largest city, is now one of the most successful economic performers in regional Australia. Newcastle's competitive advantages are many, but they can be encapsulated easily: Newcastle and the Hunter Valley marry regional cost structures with metropolitan convenience. Businesses in the region are able to take advantage of all of the services found in any of Australia's capital cities at a substantially discounted cost.

Newcastle has long been regarded as a microcosm of wider Australia with a depth and breadth of institutions and culture represented elsewhere in Australia. For many years companies introducing new products to the Australian market tested them in Newcastle first. If the trial went well in Newcastle, it was presumed it would go well elsewhere in Australia.

The Newcastle waterfont is undergoing a transformation that will make it a pleasure precinct.

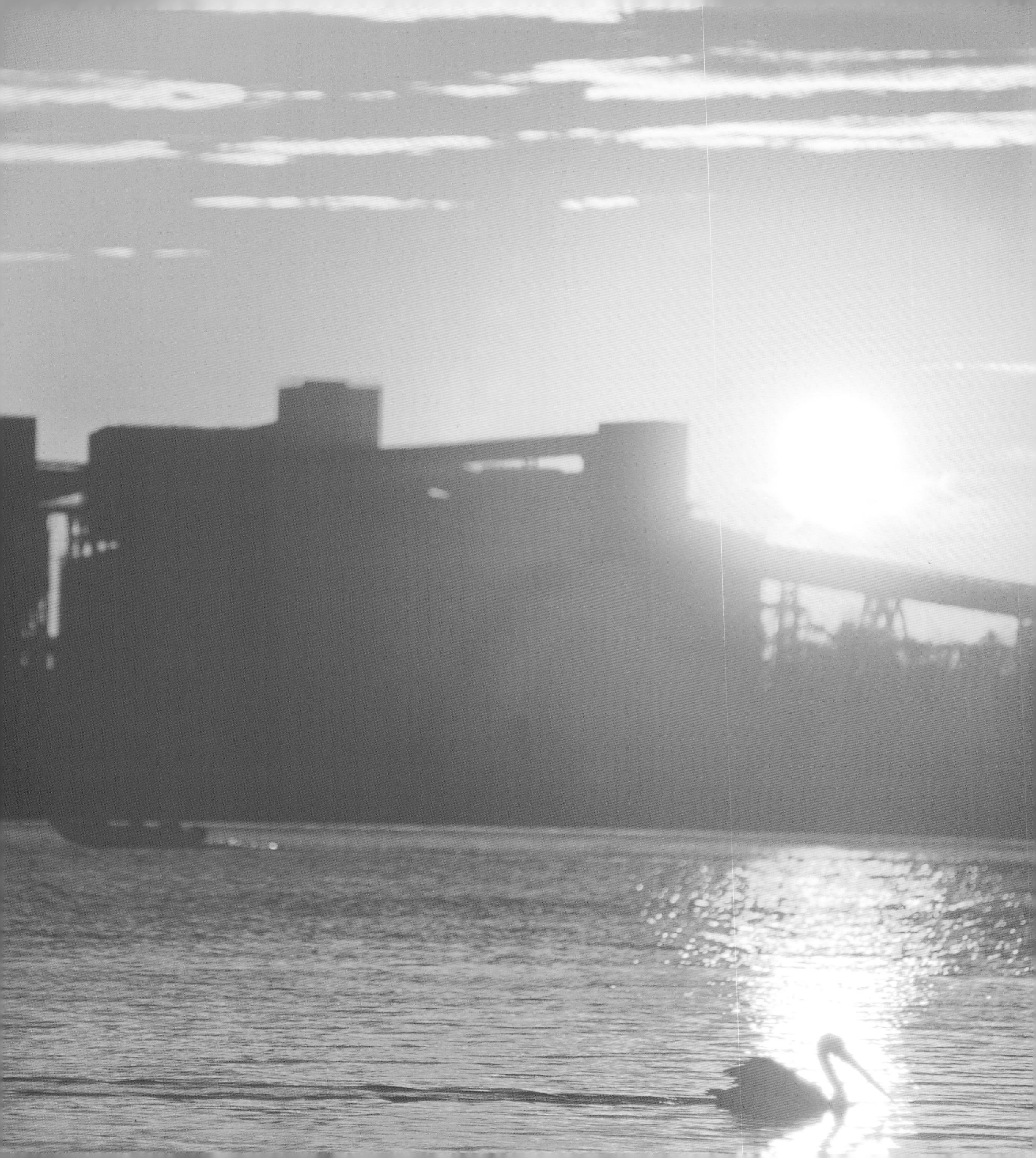

With a couple of obvious exceptions, most of Newcastle's big businesses have stayed and grown—although it's impossible to mention Newcastle without remarking on BHP's steelworks closures and decision to exit the city after eight decades.

A dramatic transition, which had its genesis in the closures, has been the merger of BHP with South African-founded, London-based Billiton plc. The new company, BHP Billiton, is dual listed, trading shares on both the Australian and London stock exchanges. The $58 million deal puts BHP Billiton in the top ranks of international resource companies.

Today, Newcastle and the Hunter Valley produce nearly 90 per cent of NSW's electricity, smelt 35 per cent of Australia's aluminium and have an export coal industry worth $5 billion a year. Alongside these natural resource industries, dominated by a handful of large employers, the region as a whole has a diversified manufacturing sector with literally thousands of small-to-medium enterprises—businesses that are increasingly recognised as the key to sustainable industry in the 21st century.

Heavy industry is still a strong earner, but 80 per cent of the region's workers are in service sector industries such as health, retail and education. Newcastle is also geared for growth in new economy businesses, which offer boundless opportunities for quick-thinking companies.

Sunset over Kooragang Island.

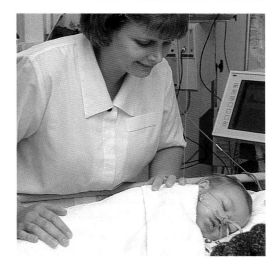

A historically strong set of transport links has matured to provide the region with quick and efficient road, rail and air transport. Newcastle is just 90 minutes drive from Sydney, which is the nation's biggest market and the first stop for the increasing numbers of multinational corporations using Australia as an Asia Pacific base.

Global commerce is more and more about finding the competitive edge, and Newcastle establishment costs are far below those of capital cities. The 15 per cent savings in operating costs that businesses can realistically expect when switching from Sydney to Newcastle is a substantial advantage in itself.

Business, government and unions have cooperated for so long now in Newcastle and the Hunter Valley region that the presence of all three groups on various regional economic boards, for example, goes without saying.

Stockton
✈ 124 Newcastle
Williamtown
Nelson Bay

WERRIBI STREET

MATER HOSPITAL ✚ →

Lambton

Below: Newcastle airport provides the region with efficient links to major cities and other regional centres.

The most recent estimate of the Hunter Valley's population—1999 figures provided by the Hunter Valley Research Foundation based on the 1996 national census—puts the number of people living in the region's 13 local government areas (LGAs) at approximately 570,000. Nearly 85 per cent of the population is concentrated in the five LGAs of the Lower Hunter Valley: Cessnock, Lake Macquarie, Maitland, Newcastle and Port Stephens.

Population changes vary from area to area, but the influx of new residents, combined with the natural birthrate, has remained for the most part easily manageable. Newcastle's proximity to Sydney offers a great opportunity to take the overflow from the NSW capital.

A substantial differential in property prices means Sydneysiders are cashing in their $1 million-plus houses in increasing numbers to buy attractive lakeside properties at about half the price.

The start-up costs for businesses, too, are well below those of Sydney. The inner Newcastle suburbs dedicated to industry are continuing to thrive, while the redevelopment of various holdings around the port, including the former steel-works site at Port Waratah, will put hundreds of hectares of prime deep-water industrial land to new and profitable uses.

Industrial developments continue to spring up in outer Newcastle suburbs and at 'greenfield' sites such as Hunter Land's Thornton estate. The $25 million

in post-BHP job creation funding provided by the NSW and federal governments and BHP has helped dozens of businesses, small and large, establish new operations in the Hunter.

Newcastle has always been high on the list for businesses looking to set up new industrial and manufacturing plants, but it is the city's gains in the 'new economy'—in service sectors, education, health and tourism—that are positioning the city for success in the 21st century.

change

The decision by BHP to close its Newcastle steel-making plant in 1999 was a make-or-break event. After years of speculation, the company made the closure announcement in April 1997, a full two years before the final closing date. BHP was lauded for giving such advance notice, as it enabled business, political and civic leaders to swing into coordinated action.

There was nothing that could be done about the thousands of steelworks jobs that would be lost, but there was plenty that could be done to influence events after the steelworks was gone.

In the period before the steelworks closure, the region's leaders banded to display the cooperation typical of the legendary Novocastrian fighting spirit.

Newcastle's coordinated lobbying efforts saw both the NSW and federal governments pour valuable job-creating resources into the area, and the leaders of other Australian regions expressed admiration for the way Newcastle marshalled its citizens to put forward its case. The evidence, both anecdotal and empirical, shows the region got it right.

Far from creating an unemployment nightmare, the steelworks closure ushered in the fastest period of employment growth in the region's recent history. Government figures show that 40,000 new jobs were created in the nine months following the steelworks closure. This rate of job creation was substantially above the national average, and by many measures the Hunter

Valley became the fastest growing job market in NSW at the time.

The new jobs were spread across a range of industries, with both full-time and part-time employment rising substantially. By early 2000 the region's workforce had risen to a level well beyond 250,000 people, a rise of almost 15 per cent in a year. Heavy industry still plays its part because of the natural resource advantages enjoyed by the region, but the economy is now overwhelmingly geared to the service sector. Today four out of every five workers are employed in the service industry and Newcastle is a shining example of a successful post-industrial economy.

City Hall is often host to business functions.

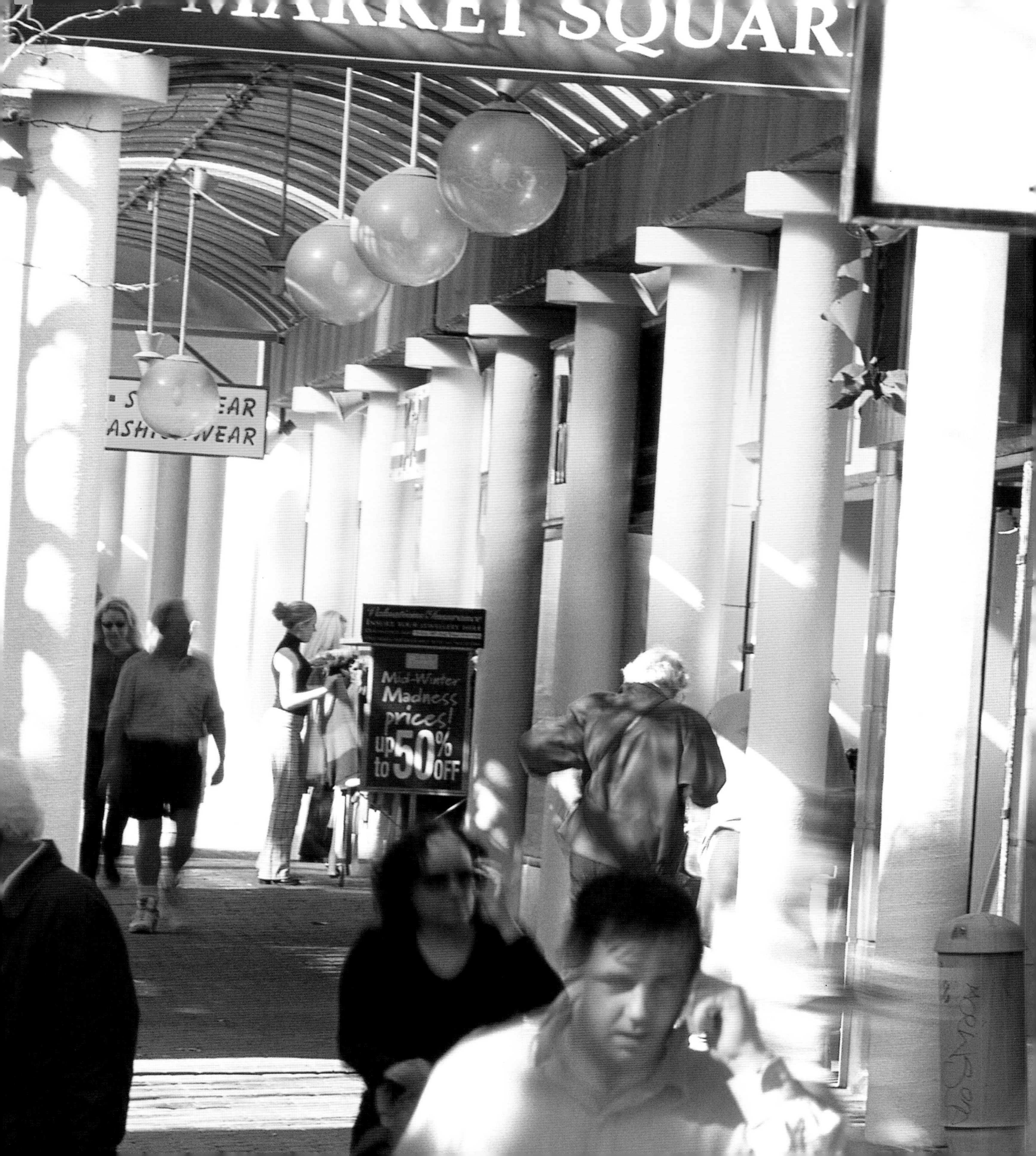
MARKET SQUAR
Mid-Winter
Madness
prices!
up to 50% OFF

Newcastle has always been high on the list for businesses looking to set up new industrial and manufacturing plants, but it is the city's gains in the 'new economy'—in service sectors, education, health and tourism—that are positioning the city for success in the 21st century.

Newcastle Mall is a popular shopping destination, catering to all consumer needs.

NEWCASTLE : BUSINESS

'We tell visitors to Newcastle "Be prepared to be surprised" because it happens all the time. People come here with perceptions that are soon blown away by our quality of life, our environment and the opportunities the city offers.'

—Councillor John S Tate, Lord Mayor, The City of Newcastle

THE CITY OF NEWCASTLE

As Australia's second oldest city, Newcastle has a rich stock of heritage buildings which lend an air of grace and dignity to the otherwise thoroughly modern city. The Customs House clock tower is just one of the city's restored and protected heritage items. The building itself is a busy European style cafe which overlooks the Harbour Foreshore Park.

Great Place, Great Lifestyle, Great Future.
Anyone who's been involved in strategic business planning knows how difficult it can be to develop a statement which accurately expresses an organisation's mission in just a few words. Ideally it has to be catchy. It also has to be relevant to all stakeholders, especially those charged with the responsibility of delivering the goods. When it's a government organisation the challenge is even greater.

Newcastle City Council's mission certainly meets these criteria. But it's more than a marketing catchphrase for glossy brochures, Council reports or business cards. It's the result of intense and focused attention on the demands of the city's natural and built heritage, the needs of current residents and creation of opportunities for coming generations of Novocastrians.

A unique combination of factors gives Newcastle—to borrow from real estate

terminology—a high location rating. The heritage residential and business precincts of the inner city adjoin surfing beaches which attract the world's best board riders in intense competition and local families just enjoying the good life.

The harbour at the mouth of the Hunter River offers easy access for bulk carriers, container ships and cargo vessels to the sea lanes of the east coast. The ships bring alumina to feed the region's smelters as well as containers and general cargoes for the growing Sydney market—the nation's biggest city—just down the freeway to the south. They sail carrying coal from the resource-rich Hunter Valley, cotton from the rich fields of the state's north-west and high-quality aluminium bound for ports around the world.

While Council encourages manufacturing and secondary industry—in a city which has

22

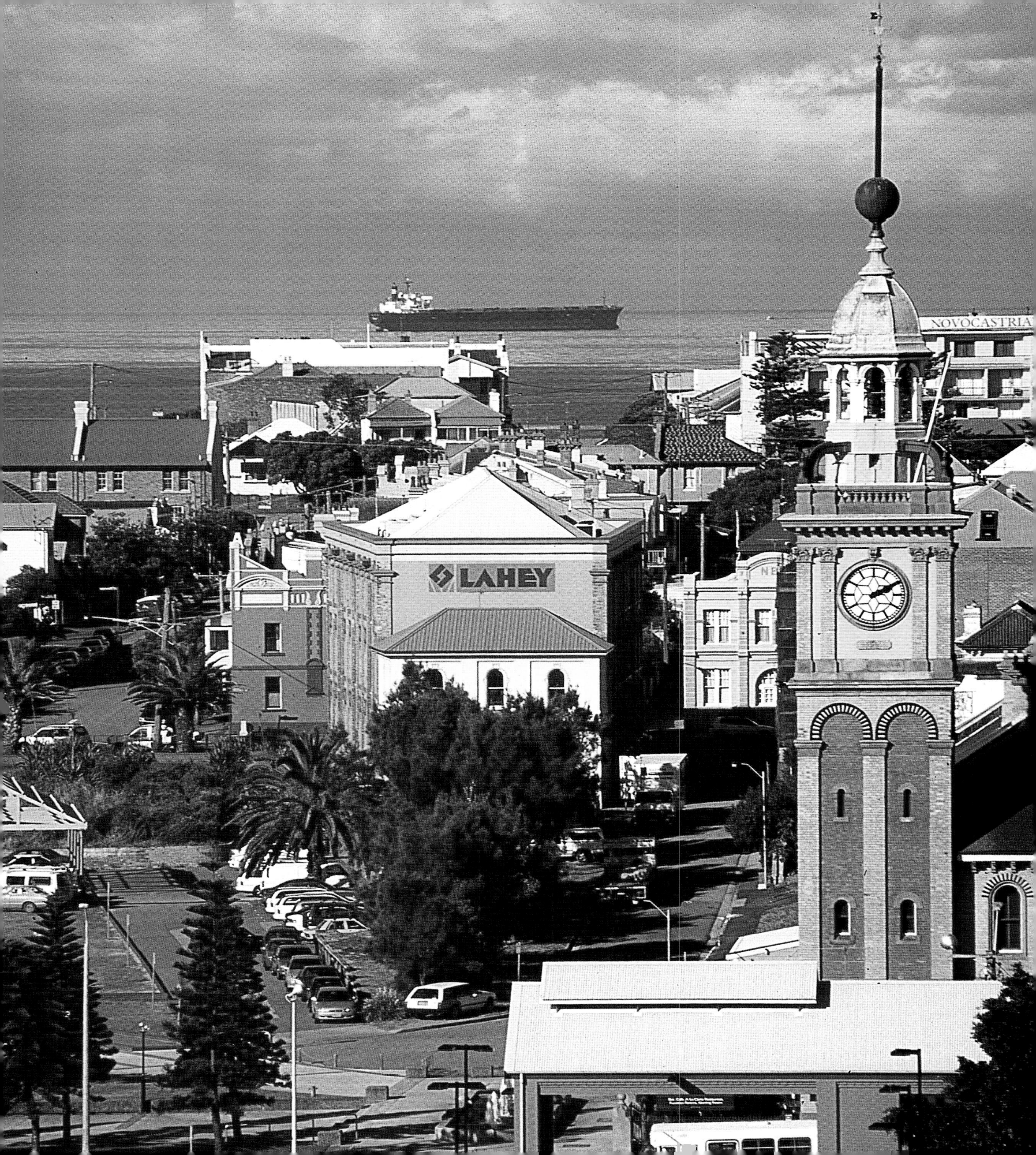
NOVOCASTRIA
LAHEY

Newcastle's deep water port played a major role in the city's development as an economic powerhouse of the nation with the world's largest coal loading terminal in the world. While maintaining its economic importance in local and national terms, the harbour is also the site of Newcastle's most obvious rebirth with Honeysuckle turning disused railway and industrial land into highly sought after residential and commercial development and a high-class marina.

long been synonymous with heavy industry—to create employment and economic growth, it's in sectors which capitalise on Newcastle's natural advantages where new jobs are being sought and created.

There are a number of reasons behind the city's continued push to establish more major hotels. With more beds the city can attract an even bigger share of the meetings business, where Newcastle has already had great success with facilities such as the restored 1500-seat Civic Theatre, the multi-purpose City Hall complex and modern performance spaces such as the Conservatorium Concert Hall. When delegates finish their conference business, they look at what the city and region has to offer and often succumb to the

temptation to return as tourists. More visitors generate more sustainable jobs.

Sustainability, in all aspects of Newcastle's ecology, economy and cultural life, is a key driving factor behind the city's actions and its plans for the future. One business unit has helped cut Council's energy usage by 30 per cent. These skills are now being marketed to authorities around Australia as well as being put to use in local developments which return power to the grid. The same team is also working to develop a greenhouse model which tracks the city's performance on greenhouse gases. With immediate feedback on environmental performance, the Council believes even further improvements can be made.

'The location of our city is probably our greatest asset: the wonderful beaches to the east; the calm waters of Lake Macquarie to the south; the water wonderland of Port Stephens to the north; and the famous Hunter vineyards and productive land of the Hunter to the west, nestled into the mountains.'

—Councillor John S Tate, Lord Mayor, The City of Newcastle

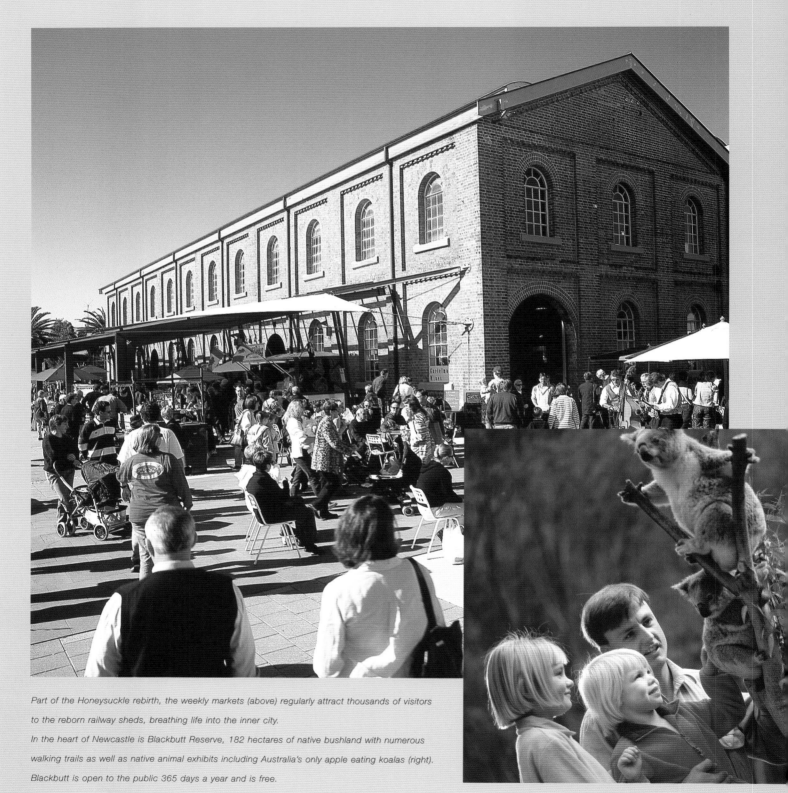

Part of the Honeysuckle rebirth, the weekly markets (above) regularly attract thousands of visitors to the reborn railway sheds, breathing life into the inner city.

In the heart of Newcastle is Blackbutt Reserve, 182 hectares of native bushland with numerous walking trails as well as native animal exhibits including Australia's only apple eating koalas (right). Blackbutt is open to the public 365 days a year and is free.

'Newcastle is a wonderful mixture of tradition, spirit and parochialism. The most important thing I have found is a willingness to embrace newcomers, new ideas and cooperate to achieve goals for the "new" Newcastle. I feel privileged to be involved in working towards a great future for this special city.'

—Janet Dore, General Manager, The City of Newcastle

Lean, green and clean. It's a far cry from the image many have of Newcastle, an image that Lord Mayor John Tate argues is further from reality every day.

'The community spirit of Newcastle has been highlighted during times such as the earthquake, but has also been reflected in the quiet but determined way the city has set about reinventing itself after the BHP moved out of steel making. In the community, in business, in all levels of government, there's a willingness to work together which is not apparent in bigger cities.

'That cooperation continues to transform the city. People are moving back to the inner suburbs, and city streets which used to slumber after business hours are alive with trendy cafes and eateries.'

A swathe of harbourside land known as Honeysuckle is being redeveloped for residential, commercial and entertainment use.

The harbour foreshore is a mecca, not only on Sundays but all week, for a stroll, a bike ride or a doze in the afternoon sun. A trek along the city beaches from the ocean baths at Merewether to the historic pool at Newcastle is known as the Bathers Way in recognition of the role played by the sea in the culture of the city.

Council also provides extensive support for the cultural life of the city. On leafy Laman Street, among the many galleries scattered throughout inner Newcastle, is the Newcastle Regional Art Gallery. Hosting regular touring exhibitions as well as the city collection, the Regional Gallery is recognised as one of the best in the nation. The Regional Museum has a matching reputation, preserving unique views of the city's past for the future.

To ensure that Novocastrian generations to come inherit a city which remains a great place with a great lifestyle, Newcastle City Council knows that it has to provide the right environment for business to invest, and that means providing professional and timely response to requests for information, advice and development proposals. General Manager Janet Dore calls it 'top value'.

'Our city has so many competitive advantages, the best thing Council can do to encourage economic growth and new business is to be the best at what we do.'

See page 173 for contact details >

two
A CENTRE FOR BUSINESS

Newcastle offers business comprehensive and well-coordinated support and marries regional costs structures with metropolitan convenience.

Newcastle and the Hunter region's competitive advantages are many, but they can be encapsulated in a single statement: the region marries regional cost structures with metropolitan convenience. Newcastle Airport at Williamtown connects directly with Australia's three east-coast state capitals, as well as the ACT, and international visitors can be in Newcastle less than an hour after arriving in Sydney.

Businesses moving to the region are able to take advantage of all of the services found in any of Australia's capital cities, but at substantially discounted costs. The region's 13 local councils work together through the Hunter Region Organisation of Councils (HROC), which fosters cooperation and resource sharing between members and encourages investment in the region.

Development costs in Newcastle are substantially below those in the capital cities. Commercial, industrial and high-quality residential land is all priced attractively. More importantly, Newcastle's manageable scale means even new greenfield sites are available within minutes of the central business district and adjacent to transport and infrastructure routes.

One of Newcastle's most important land development projects is Steel River. Adjacent to the Port of Newcastle, Steel River boasts a number of Australian firsts. The NSW government passed special provisions to the State Planning Act guaranteeing development applications for conforming businesses

'With its highly skilled workforce, first-class infrastructure, high-quality telecommunications networks and abundant water and electricity supply, the Hunter is ready to face the challenges of the 21st century.'

—The Hon Bob Carr, New South Wales Premier and Minister for the Arts

One of the landmark glass office blocks on Wharf Road, home to a range of government departments and business support organisations.

are approved within 28 days. The Australian federal government also enacted legislation in 1999 that allows Steel River to operate as a free trade zone, so that materials imported to create goods for export do not incur customs and excise duties.

The Port of Newcastle is Australia's biggest tonnage cargo port and a range of new facilities, including the proposed multi-purpose terminal HubPort on the former steelworks site, will expand upon an already dynamic trade. Local business leaders, in many cases working closely with the region's pro-active development bodies and industry clusters, are well attuned to modern export culture. Ninety per cent of the Port of Newcastle's business is in export trade and while every effort is made to increase imports, exports are now worth a booming $5 billion annually. The Hunter Valley only claims nine per cent of NSW's population, but it produces more than 32 per cent of its exports.

Business support in Newcastle is comprehensive and well coordinated. A range of government and private sector lobby groups, peak bodies and regional support organisations work together in a regional network to strengthen Newcastle's economic and industrial clout.

One of the most important addresses for investors coming to Newcastle is 237–251 Wharf Road, a pair of almost identical modern three-storey buildings overlooking the harbour. Built in the

1980s by one of Newcastle's premier building companies, the Doran Group, these landmark glass twins are home to a range of government departments, support organisations and public corporations. The Premier's Department, federal Senator John Tierney, the Hunter Economic Development Corporation (HEDC), the Department of State and Regional Development (DSRD), Honeysuckle Development Corporation, the Rail Infrastructure Corporation and others, all operate from these buildings.

Left: The refurbished T&G building on Hunter Street.

Businesses need to know that professional support in all its guises is available promptly and efficiently. Newcastle's growing service sector includes representatives of most of the big law and accounting firms, such as Ferrier Hodgson and PricewaterhouseCoopers.

Most of the major financial institutions have substantial operations in the city, and a new source of capital has been available in the form of the rejuvenated Newcastle Stock Exchange. Backed with federal government funding, the exchange is pitched at smaller enterprises such as building societies, credit unions and investment syndicates.

High-quality IT and telecommunications firms are an increasingly important part of Newcastle's economic growth. The region is serviced by all of the major telecommunications firms together with an ever-burgeoning number of emerging carriers offering the full range of telephony and high-speed broadband services.

The region's population has proven to be enthusiastic users of Internet services with connection rates well above the national average. As well as the national and international service providers, a range of home-grown companies such as Hunternet and Nobbys Net are building market share with a combination of competitive rates and local knowledge.

Above: Renovated terraces around the court house and police station are home to law firms.

unions

The Hunter Valley has a progressive, cooperative approach to industrial relations. Unions are regularly involved at the highest levels of regional planning, but the Australian federal government's Workplace Relations Act means union membership is now a matter of individual choice. Larger employers tend to work closely with the unions, while many of the region's small to medium enterprises have very little contact with them. Unionised workplaces are increasingly operating under enterprise bargaining agreements, although many continue on the award system, which was recently streamlined by the federal government.

Newcastle's unions work together under the auspices of the Newcastle Trades Hall Council, which works closely with the NSW Labor Council, and the ACTU (Australian Council of Trade Unions). Large industrial projects in the Hunter Valley are generally operated with union involvement with all parties working to deliver projects on time and on budget.

While the region's employment profile is changing, industry is still a major provider of jobs.

Water charges have fallen by a third in real terms over the past decade.

utilities

Basic infrastructure services—including power, water and gas—in the Hunter are all world-class and competitively priced. Three state-owned generating companies, Eraring Energy, Delta Electricity and Macquarie Generation, are based in the region, together with 'niche' producers such as Redbank Power Station and a growing host of renewable energy sites.

Newcastle City Council is receiving international recognition for energy efficiencies won through the Australian Municipal Energy Improvement Facility (AMEIF), which provides a range of services and advice to businesses and industry wanting to save on power costs.

User-pays principles are increasingly accepted in water usage, but Newcastle can claim a national first. Hunter Water, which in 1982 became the first utility to introduce user pays tariffs, replaced the then-universal system of charging on the basis of land value.

Water consumption has fallen by about 30 per cent since that time, and for most of the past decade, Hunter Water customers have had the lowest household water use in the nation. Hunter Water was corporatised in 1992 and ongoing efficiencies as a result of restructuring have seen water charges fall by a third in real terms.

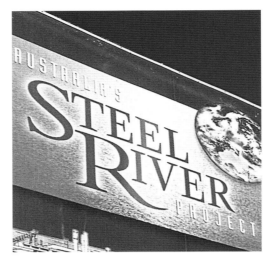

With an experienced staff and an influential voice in government, the HEDC is involved in formulating major economic strategies for the region.

The HEDC offers assistance to companies that want to invest in the region and it can:

- liaise with state and local government;
- provide contacts with Hunter industry networks and suppliers;
- compile lists of available development sites;
- profile staff and salary levels;
- provide familiarisation help for staff and management; and
- assist with information for feasibility studies.

In recognition of the rapid change affecting the regional economy, the HEDC has established a Hunter Futures Committee to explore the possibilities of innovation.

The HEDC is the key driver of the various Hunter Advantage policies, but the DSRD is often the first point of contact within government for companies wishing to do business in the region. By adopting a 'one-stop-shop' policy, the department works to allow business to have an efficient and effective relationship with government. The department administers at least 10 major regional NSW programs including the Business Retention and Expansion Program, the Regional Economic Transition Scheme and the Developing Regional Resources program.

Taking a leading hand in Newcastle's development is the Department of Urban Affairs and Planning (DUAP). Part of its brief includes the management of growth and change in the greater metropolitan region, which runs from the Illawarra through Sydney to the Hunter. DUAP works with developers and local government on large-scale projects, such as Honeysuckle, to ensure a more sustainable approach is taken.

Sustainable development looks beyond the traditional economic bottom line to include a range of social and environmental elements that form the 'triple bottom line'.

Newcastle City Council is leading the nation in sustainability and is encouraging the broader community to recognise its importance. Working with Canberra think tank the Australia Institute, the council has developed indicators to measure the city's progress. Newcastle's sustainability criteria are:

- air quality;
- cleanliness of beaches;
- quality of community space;
- educational opportunities;
- levels of unemployment;
- appropriate transport networks;
- conservation of local native plants and animals;
- consumption of resources;
- availability of appropriate housing for everyone; and
- diversity of employment and industry sectors.

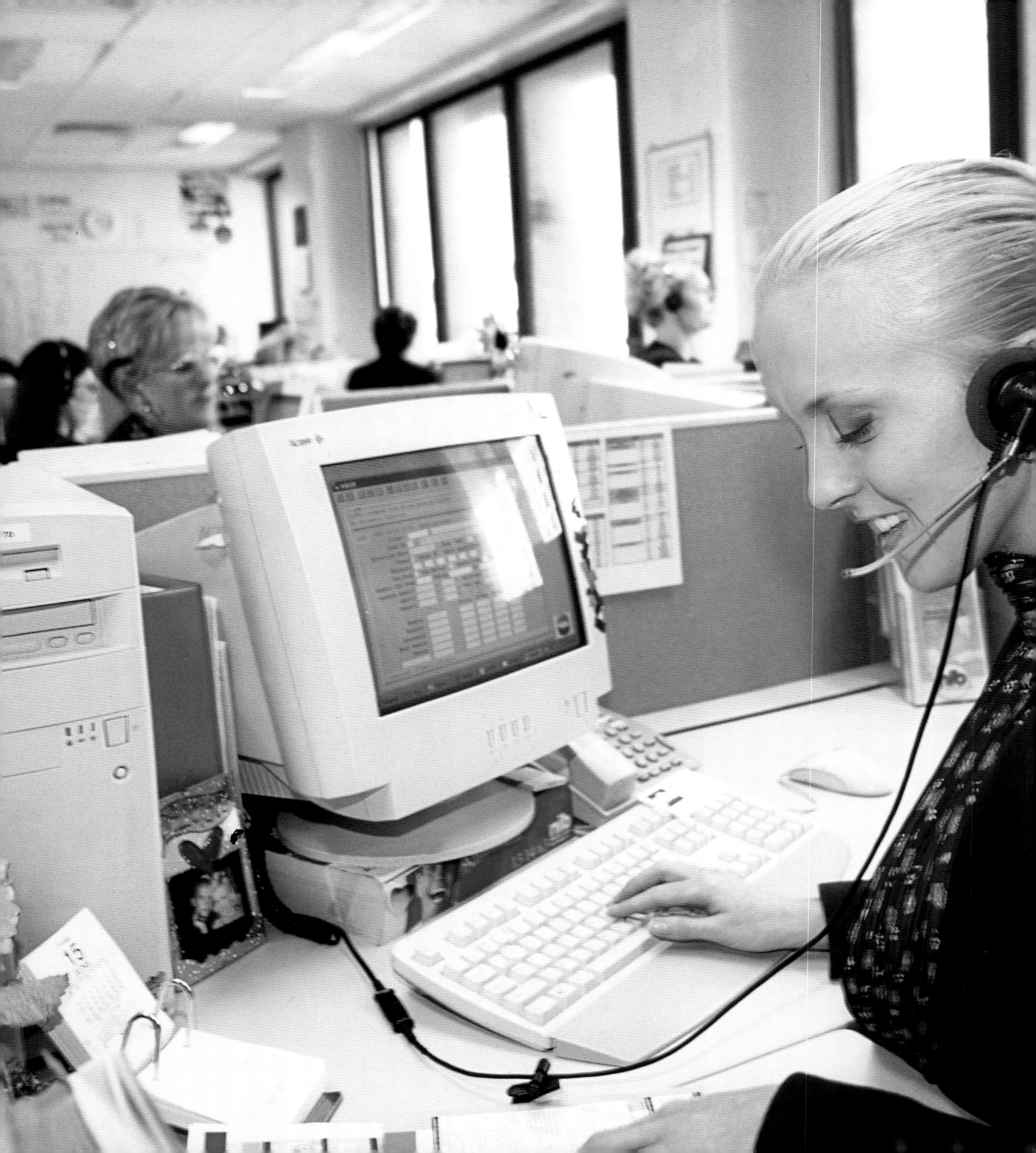

at call

Newcastle business leaders have worked hard to take advantage of the dynamic growth in call centres. The HEDC receives a steady flow of inquiries about the Hunter's call centre potential and has led the region's investment drive. Its executive officer, Gillian Summers, says Newcastle has a number of competitive advantages, including a sound telecommunications infrastructure, keenly priced commercial land and buildings, and a literate, flexible workforce.

At least 2,000 jobs were created in Newcastle call centres by early 2001. Companies including Australian Wine Selectors, insurers NIB and AAMI, and EnergyAustralia all set up in the city. NIB began with a small office employing three staff in Newcastle's Hunter Street; it now employs 80.

One of the most exciting prospects is a Commonwealth Bank call centre planned for the Newcastle CBD with an estimated 150 jobs on offer in its first stage. Also, the New South Wales (NSW) Police Infringement Processing Bureau's centre is planning to move from Parramatta to Maitland, creating 150 jobs, lured, Gillian Summers says, by a large, stable workforce and lower establishment costs.

'These new companies are footloose in their nature, and the Hunter has a number of incentives with which to attract them,' she says.

NIB call centre, one of a growing number of call centres making the region home.

'Newcastle is an area with a lot of skill and potential, and with the right vision there is an awful lot that we can achieve. When it comes down to it, there aren't too many other places that combine the work and lifestyle opportunities that we have here.'

—Jeff Phillips, Managing Director, Varley Group

'The Newcastle Permanent is a large local mutual financial institution with our financial strength derived from the support of our strong regional community over many years. I am confident of a dynamic and bright future for our region and we look forward to playing a significant role in this future as the complete financial services provider.'

—Howard Frith, Managing Director, Newcastle Permanent Building Society Limited

NEWCASTLE PERMANENT BUILDING SOCIETY LIMITED

Newcastle Permanent Building Society, an independent, mutual financial organisation, has a long and close association with the Newcastle and Hunter communities.

The Society's origins began in Newcastle in 1903 and it is now the largest and financially strongest building society in Australia. With assets exceeding $2.2 billion and more than 500 staff, the Society plays a major role in the region's economy. We have grown with the region to become a trusted name in financial services with a reputation for friendly, efficient service; affordable finance packages; and secure, market competitive investment products.

Legislative change, technology and development, and enhancement of our range of products and services as well as our branch, lending and business facilities enables the Society to operate as a complete financial services provider. The Society offers the

Hunter and Central Coast people a genuine alternative for their banking services.

Home and land lending are central to our business, however, the Society's range of financial services and products also includes:

- *Credit facilities—credit card, personal loans, lines of credit and overdrafts*
- *Mortgage loans—fixed, variable and introductory rates: one loan and mortgage minimisation*
- *Business banking services—overdrafts, business loans, guarantees*
- *Savings accounts—passbook and statement*
- *Investment accounts—fixed interest or variable rates: on call or fixed*
- *Specialty accounts—children's accounts, Xmas Club and 60Plus*
- *Transaction accounts—ATM cards, debit Visa, and cheque facilities*

Opposite, from top: Newcastle Permanent Building Society Head Office, a symbol of the region's strength and security; The Society has a reputation for friendly, efficient customer service and a very strong bond with the people of the region.

- *Financial planning—superannuation, managed funds, allocated pension*
- *Insurance—house and contents, car, mortgage and loan protection*
- *Internet and phone banking, including BPay*
- *Foreign cash and Travellers cheques*

Our products and services are complemented by the largest branch network in the region. This strong presence allows efficient face-to-face service, serving over 50,000 people daily—the Society is committed to meeting members' needs.

Over many years, a strong bond has developed between the Society and the people of the region. Our support for a variety of community based regional initiatives is one of the ways in which this bond is nurtured. From major sponsorships, such as our Partnership for Life with the Breast Cancer Institute of Australia and our support for the Hunter Medical Research Foundation, to a host of smaller community based initiatives and programs, the Society is proud of its role in helping to enrich the quality of life for the community.

Newcastle Permanent is a large employer with more than 500 staff drawn from the local community—further strengthening our regional presence and the relationship between the Society and its members. The Society is proud of its long history of support for the region and looks forward to playing a significant role in the region's future growth.

NEWCASTLE BUSINESS

See page 180 for contact details >

'The key factor in the success of Websters Australia is quality assurance. We have taken that principle and followed it through every aspect of our operation, from training to recruitment, and all our field activities, including corporate and security protection, emergency and medical management and facilities management.'

—Phillip Egge, Managing Director, Websters Australia Pty Ltd

WEBSTERS AUSTRALIA PTY LTD

Training for a Secure Future

Websters Australia was among the first to recognise the need for a high standard of training in the Security Industry and Workplace Health and Safety. Now Websters Training Academy provides training in fields as varied as security, investigations, emergency services, risk management, workplace occupational health and safety, workplace assessment and training and fire technology.

As the security industry is one of the fastest-growing service sectors in the world, Websters Managing Director Phillip Egge was quick to understand that a lack of recognised quality training would limit growth, and the reputation of those working in the business.

Websters Australia decided to take on the responsibility of developing and operating training courses to meet the growing demand. As well as mainstream security and investigative skills, the Websters curriculum includes courses in the workplace occupational health and safety law and risk management. The range of course topics reflects the comprehensive approach taken by Websters Australia. 'Websters is a knowledge business, and our training programs impart that depth of knowledge and experience,' says Phillip Egge.

This page: Websters Training Academy.

Opposite, from top: Websters staff are highly trained in all aspects of emergency services; Websters Australia management team.

As well as the major training centres in Newcastle, Parramatta, Brisbane and the Gold Coast, other Websters facilities around the nation also have training facilities. High-quality training with guaranteed standards ensures a supply of well-qualified staff for other Websters national and global businesses.

Security and Workplace Safety

Websters Australia Managing Director Phillip Egge believes that 'security' also means safety for employees, patrons, clients and the public. That is why the innovative approach taken by the company has driven its expansion around the nation, with the provision of services as varied as emergency planning and disaster recovery, fraud analysis and protection.

From its headquarters in Newcastle and from offices in most state capitals, Websters provides a wide range of services to Australian companies, including close personal protection for executives in high-risk locations, alarm monitoring, static guards, and workplace health and safety audits.

As the diversity of risk exposure increases, Websters believes a proactive approach offers the best protection. The provision of security officers at a major industrial site, for example, is not just to protect property, and keep people out, but to ensure a secure work environment for employees and the health and safety of visitors.

With over 50 years experience, Websters Australia uses the latest technology to ensure its services are at the cutting edge. The core values of trust, honesty and integrity, however, remain unchanged. Websters Australia is also making inroads into the lucrative markets in the US, Europe and Asia, where the company is confident its comprehensive approach and no-fuss attitude will help it win new global clients.

See page 189 for contact details >

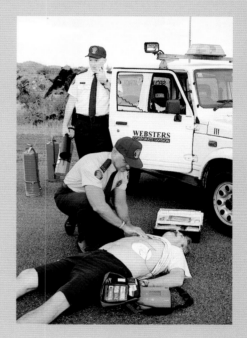

'NIB Health Funds is an important part of the Hunter's social and economic fabric. We provide first-class health care for members, and support initiatives that make a contribution to improved health and lifestyle in the wider community. Above all, NIB's business growth from our Hunter headquarters is one of the region's true success stories.'

—Colin Rogers, Managing Director, NIB Health Funds Ltd

NIB HEALTH FUNDS LTD

NIB is one of Australia's strongest health insurers and one of the top four funds in NSW. In short, it is a Hunter region success story.

The fund began in 1952 in BHP's Newcastle Steel Works, operating from an office at the gates of BHP. In 1962, it transferred to Hunter Street, which remains headquarters for an organisation that now has a footprint across Australia.

NIB presently maintains a branch network throughout New South Wales and the Australian Capital Territory, Queensland, Victoria and South Australia.

The NIB group of companies, which includes NIB Dental and Eye Care Centres and NIB Private Hospital, provides employment for almost 800 full-time and part-time staff and health cover for more than 500,000 Australians.

NIB starts the new millennium in its strongest ever position, with reserves well in excess of the Federal Government's required statutory levels, and a diverse and highly successful range of services complementing core health care products.

NIB remains a partner for many of the region's business groups, a strong advocate for the Hunter in state and national markets, and a successful example of achieving sustained business growth from a Newcastle base.

In addition, NIB's award-winning Call Centre operation is being used as a marketing tool by peak development bodies seeking to position the Hunter as a leader in the Call Centre industry.

See page 181 for contact details >

SHARP ELECTRONICS
OFFICE NATIONAL

'Sharp Electronics Office National, a local company of 30 years, supplying Business Equipment Solutions, believes the Hunter region certainly is a great "Centre for Business". Newcastle is a diversified business centre, has always embraced changes in new technology, and adapts well to an ever-changing market. Our growth and success stems from our ability to provide innovative solutions and excellent after sales service.'

—Ben Hickson, General Manager, Sharp Electronics Office National

See page 185 for contact details >

'Sparke Helmore is an energetic, innovative and progressive law firm with a clear and focused vision for the future. Founded in Newcastle and through strategic placement of offices in Newcastle, Muswellbrook, Sydney, Melbourne, Canberra, Brisbane and Adelaide, the firm meets the high standards and volumes of work demanded by the government, business and insurance sectors in the major economic centres of Australia.'

—Paul Anicich, Partner, Sparke Helmore Solicitors

SPARKE HELMORE SOLICITORS

Sparke Helmore first opened its doors in Newcastle in 1882. While it now offers innovative and commercial solutions to insurers, government and business throughout Australia, its Newcastle office provided the base from which it established its position as one of the country's leading firms.

Twenty nine partners and over 400 professional and support staff provide comprehensive legal services in Australia's major state capitals and economic centres of Sydney, Melbourne, Brisbane, Adelaide and in Canberra, the national capital.

The Firm continues to provide a premier service to Newcastle and the Hunter Region through its founding office and another in the regional centre of Muswellbrook.

Sparke Helmore's team of specialists operate in the fields of corporate and business law, construction and engineering, employment and occupational health and safety, general liability, planning, local government and the environment, property and infrastructure, technology law and compensation and insurance.

The Firm has built a solid and extensive expertise in resources and energy law, particularly through its Newcastle office, which has been highly responsive to the economic framework and needs of Newcastle and Hunter Region.

Sparke Helmore's exceptional service, timely advice and ability to achieve practical outcomes set it apart in the competitive environment in which it operates.

The Firm's strong growth is directly related to its ability to respond to the changing circumstances of the business sectors it services.

See page 186 for contact details >

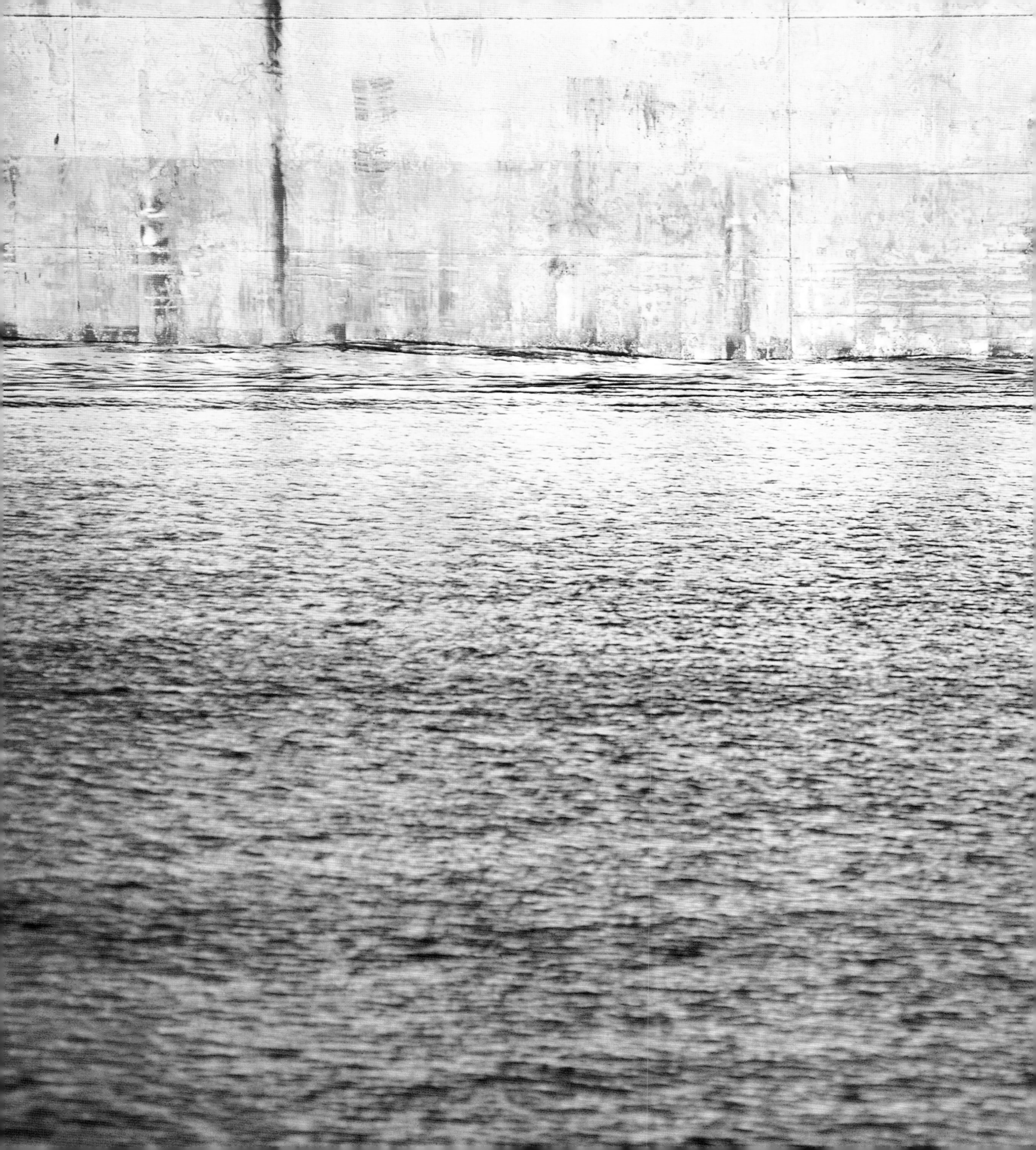

three
GROWING STRENGTH

Newcastle is aware
of the need for continual change and improvement, and the rise of industry clusters has helped it take the lead in areas such as new media, information technology, wine and aquaculture.

'The need for new skills and knowledge is not confined to young people. We all need to continuously update our skills to stay abreast of job changes and adapt as industries and occupations change.'

—Gaye Hart, Director, Hunter Institute of Technology—TAFE NSW

clusters

In Newcastle and the Hunter, a new generation of 'smart' companies are taking the plunge and coming up with results. Some of these new industries remain in the manufacturing field, while others are more service or process oriented. The leaders of these industries are aware of the need for continual change and improvement.

The Hunter Economic Development Corporation (HEDC) has encouraged the shift from low-cost, high-volume mass production, to knowledge-intensive, flexible specialisation that competes on quality as well as price. There has also been a rise of industry

networks or 'clusters', in which otherwise small companies band together to gain economies of scale, while retaining the flexibility that comes from being small companies. Clusters also allow companies to procure contracts and projects that would otherwise be beyond their grasp.

One of the advocates of clustering is former Newcastle University academic Professor Roy Green, who says: 'In a region once disproportionately dependent on a few big manufacturers, enterprises with fewer than 80 employees now account for more than 90 per cent of Hunter manufacturing jobs.'

Funded by a grant from BHP's Development Trust, agencies led by the HEDC, the Hunter Regional Development Organisation (HURDO) and the Industry Development Centre (IDC) set to work identifying industry clusters likely to succeed in the region.

Clusters in areas such as agriculture, arts, biotechnology, building, defence, education, energy, engineering, equine, health services and research, information technology, marine, metal products, mining, sustainable development, tourism and wine were the result and now boast membership of hundreds of Hunter Valley companies.

The Hunter Area Consultative Committee has also funded a number of business plans in recent years, concentrating on new and developing industries. These government agencies work closely with the university and institute of technology sectors, and with private sector industry organisations such as the Newcastle and Hunter Business Chamber, as well as industry clusters.

It is this across the board determination to focus on industry sectors that has given Newcastle and the Hunter region a competitive advantage and many recent successes.

The most established industry network is HunterNet, an engineering and manufacturing group with more than 25 long-standing members with combined sales approaching $200 million. One of HunterNet's founders is Waratah Engineering managing director Joss de Iuliis, who says networking has helped his company more than double its turnover.

There have been many other successes in the region that have occurred well away from the glare of mainstream media scrutiny. A perfect example is mission:DynamicMedia, which supplied sophisticated film editing software used in the hit films *Blair Witch Project* and *Titanic*. Operating in the light industrial areas around the Newcastle suburb of Hamilton, mission:DynamicMedia is just one of a brace of companies involved in the region's IT and media industries.

Film is a growing industry for Newcastle and the Hunter, a factor recognised by the federal government when the Hunter Area Consultative Committee helped establish the Newcastle and Hunter Film and Television Office. Project manager June Tayloe says Newcastle is an increasingly attractive location for large-scale national and international film crews.

'What we offer is access. You can get six semitrailers of gear in and out of Newcastle without a problem and that's not always easy, and we have a fee structure that's as competitive as they come. Films like *Young Einstein* and *Bootmen* have put Newcastle on the map. We aim to keep it there,' she says.

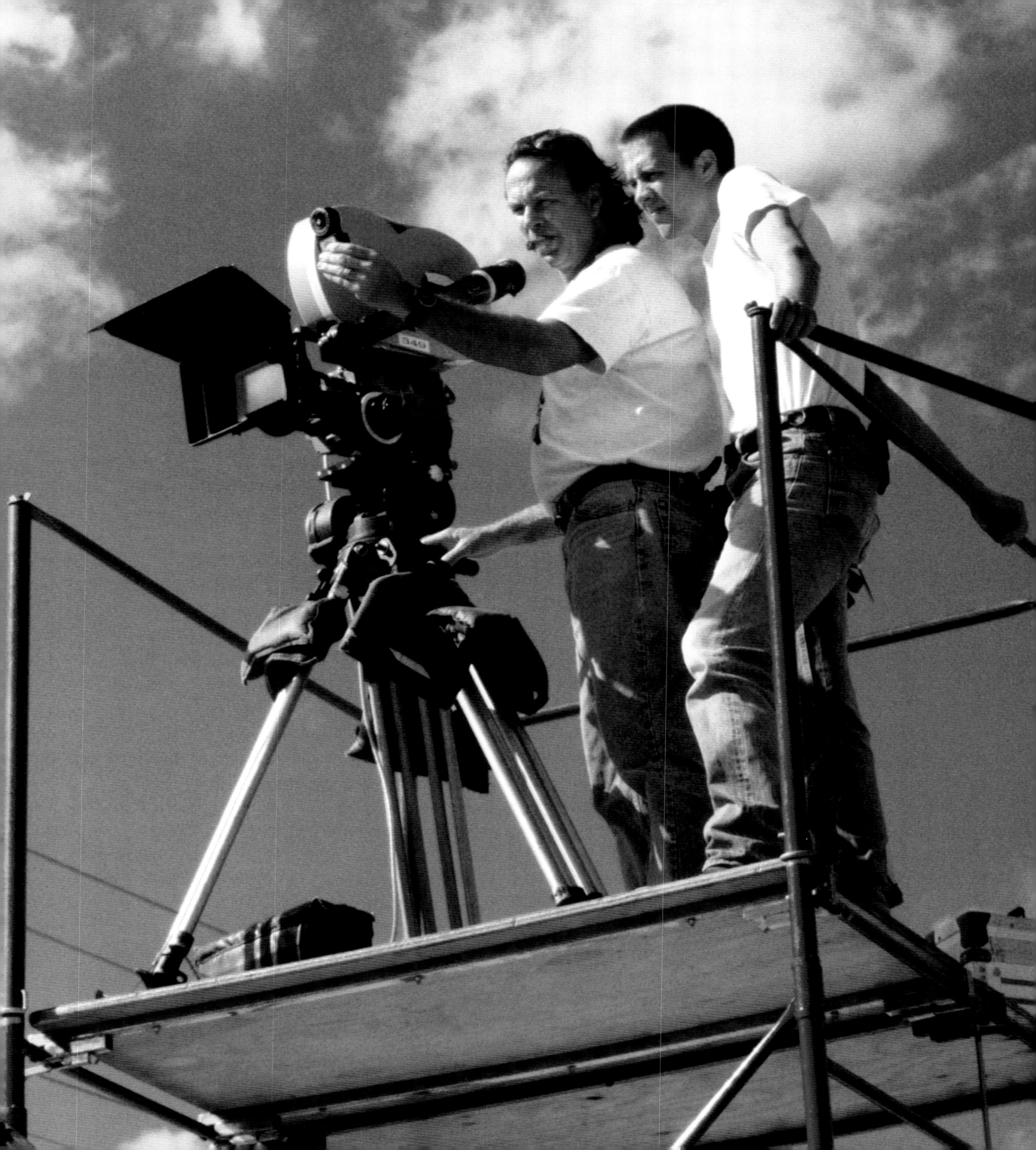

Throughout the CBD, refurbished offices and new apartment blocks are bringing people back to the heart of the city.

HunterTech, the region's information technology (IT) cluster, is at the centre of an exciting phase of growth. Business development manager Peter O'Malley says HunterTech's membership has grown dramatically since its inception in November 1998 and he expects it to continue expanding as the region's IT industry gains size and maturity.

Of the100 or so IT businesses in the Hunter, more than 60 are members of HunterTech. HunterTech members employ about 2,500 people, and the industry overall accounts for about 3,500 jobs in the region.

The growth in IT is happening relatively unnoticed as there is no large infrastructure or plants that make it stand out. Technology Partners is an example of the region's quiet success. The company pulled off the IT equivalent of selling coal to Newcastle by securing a crucial contract with California's Silicon Valley in early 2001.

Technology Partners is just one of a growing number of companies attracted to Newcastle as a cost-effective alternative to Sydney's IT hot spots. 'The competitive office rentals and property prices, the lower wage structures, the steady flow of highly trained graduates from the university are all here. And having half of your IT industry working together in an organisation like HunterTech allows small operators to punch way up out of their weight. They get the critical mass they need by working with other HunterTech members,' Peter O'Malley says.

He also believes that the region's civic and business leaders know that a strong, innovative IT sector is needed if Newcastle is going to match its industrial age achievements in the new information age. 'The pace of change all around the world is increasing all the time and ... we need to drive home to people the need to be innovative and to use our brains as well as our natural resources.

'I know that with Hunter companies like Computer Systems Australia, Advanced Systems Integration, Hunter Control and Advitech, we're well and truly on the right track,' he says.

Newcastle businessman Chris Deere set up Internet service provider HunterLink in 1996. It was the right company at the right time and its client list quickly grew to include hundreds of the region's most prominent businesses and organisations. HunterLink helped introduce more than its share of technophobe executives to the joys of the Internet.

HunterLink soon attracted the interest of international investors, and was taken over in July 2000 by Singapore-based Pacific Internet (Australia).

Chris Deere formed a new business, Ipera, which was again in the right place at the right time. In its first year Ipera set about building a multi-million-dollar high-speed broadband fibre-optic loop around the Newcastle central business district (CBD).

'We have seven kilometres of underground fibre-optic cable throughout the city and we are able to provide that service at a cost comparable to capital cities,' Chris Deere says. 'Previously, regional users, if they had the service at all, would have had to pay two or three times the rate of users in Sydney or Melbourne.'

The cable network means every business in the Newcastle CBD can be connected to a cost-effective system giving them very high-speed Internet access and low-cost telephony, Chris Deere says.

'This is extremely important to the city in many ways and it is a major benefit in our drive to attract more call centres.'

The bigger Hunter wineries—Drayton, McGuigan, Rosemount, Rothbury, Tulloch and Tyrrells—are household names. The descendants of the pioneer families who gave their name to many of these now big businesses remain in the industry.

Rosemount Estate founder Bob Oatley established his company in 1968 on a property flanking the Hunter River at Muswellbrook. The company sprang to national prominence in the late 1970s when former New South Wales Premier Neville Wran described Rosemount chardonnay as his favourite tipple.

In one of the biggest wine stock market plays of recent years, Australian company Southcorp Ltd gained a place among the world's top 10 winemakers with a $1.5 billion acquisition of the Oatley family's Rosemount Estate.

Research repeatedly shows that wine is the Hunter Valley's single most potent image. The Hunter is Australia's oldest wine-growing district and the undisputed cellar capital is the once sleepy village of Pokolbin, a short drive from Cessnock.

Pokolbin alone boasts more than 50 wineries with dozens of resorts and bed-and-breakfast establishments scattered throughout the rolling vine-covered hills. These few square kilometres turn out some of the world's best semillons, and Hunter varietal chardonnay and pinot noir were first national, and now international, success stories.

Nowadays, Pokolbin is one of the most popular destinations for overnight and weekend travel from Sydney. Package tours between wineries, resorts and restaurants mean first-time travellers are shown the best of Pokolbin's food, drink and scenery.

Technology is the unsung hero behind Pokolbin's success. Purists might turn up their noses, but modern methods and materials hold the key to the Hunter Valley's consistently high-quality vintages. Winemaking is a science as much as an art and the Valley's big winemakers have spent millions of dollars installing high-tech processing, fermentation and storage facilities. The availability of this efficient, cost-effective winemaking infrastructure

means growers from around the country send their grapes to the Hunter Valley for crushing. The region now processes more than twice its grown tonnage every season.

In the past, the predominantly dry climate has caused water shortages for the valley's vignerons, but a 4,500 megalitre pipeline from the Hunter River to Pokolbin is transforming irrigation practices in the region. Championed by leading winemaker Brian McGuigan, the $7 million Pokolbin pipeline has already begun to noticeably improve yields for participating winemakers who can now expand their plantings with certainty.

Agriculture in the Hunter earns the region more than $280 million a year and employs more than 6,500 people working an estimated 1.5 million hectares. Most of the region's producers look to local and national markets, but an increasing number are basing their businesses on exports, particularly to South-East Asia.

Beef is the Hunter's biggest primary industry earner, followed by poultry, milk, grapes, wool, pasture crops, eggs, pigs and wheat. Measured in terms of farm numbers and herd sizes, the Hunter Valley's dairy industry is in decline. The region's main processing plant, Dairy

Farmers at Hexham, however, has the critical mass required to survive deregulation and looks set for an assured future.

New crops such as herbs, olives, soybeans and a range of Asian vegetables are increasingly popular crops, often on farms that were once given over to dairy farming. Consumers have shown they are prepared to pay a premium for goods with certifiable organic credentials, and more and more farmers are opting to grow these products. The area under certified, chemical-free production is increasing. Proximity to Sydney is likely to drive further organic farming developments.

Hunter Valley wineries process more than twice the region's grown tonnage every year.

The Upper Hunter is one of the world's great racehorse breeding regions.

breeding

Scone, in the Upper Hunter Valley, is one of the world's great racehorse breeding regions. The transfer of 'shuttle' stallions between the northern and southern hemispheres has led to huge improvements in bloodstock genetics. Some of the world's great stallions spend a season each year at the Upper Hunter's world-class studs. Scone TAFE boasts one of the world's most advanced equine study centres, an $18 million establishment.

Farm based tourism is another niche growth area. Farm stay bed-and-breakfast accommodation, a long-established pursuit in the UK, for example, can provide valuable farm-gate income.

Development of aquaculture in the region is helping to ease the pressure on natural fish stocks.

fisheries

The Hunter's waterways, especially the north arm of the Hunter River and Port Stephens, have long been home to substantial oyster industries. Recent figures indicate the Hunter produces about one-third of the state's favourite oyster, the Sydney Rock, and it is also the base for a new industry, the Pacific Oyster. All up, the Hunter's oyster leases cover a substantial 1,300 hectares.

Pressure on natural fish stocks has led to rapid development of aquaculture with live fish shipments to Sydney and then on to South-East Asia a distinct possibility. Helped by state government researchers at the Port Stephens Fisheries Centre, Taylors Beach, the region's fisheries are quick to pick up new marketing and production methods.

Rob McCormack's company Crayhaven is one of aquaculture's biggest success stories. Crayhaven produces about 30 species of yabbies, prawns, fish and eels. He says the industry is expanding steadily but surely. 'We were one of the first, but there are now hundreds of aquaculture businesses in the state, and probably 30 or 40 here in the Hunter.

'I have no doubt aquaculture will continue to do well here. We have perfect soils, reliable and clean water, a great climate and we're close to the major markets,' Rob McCormack says.

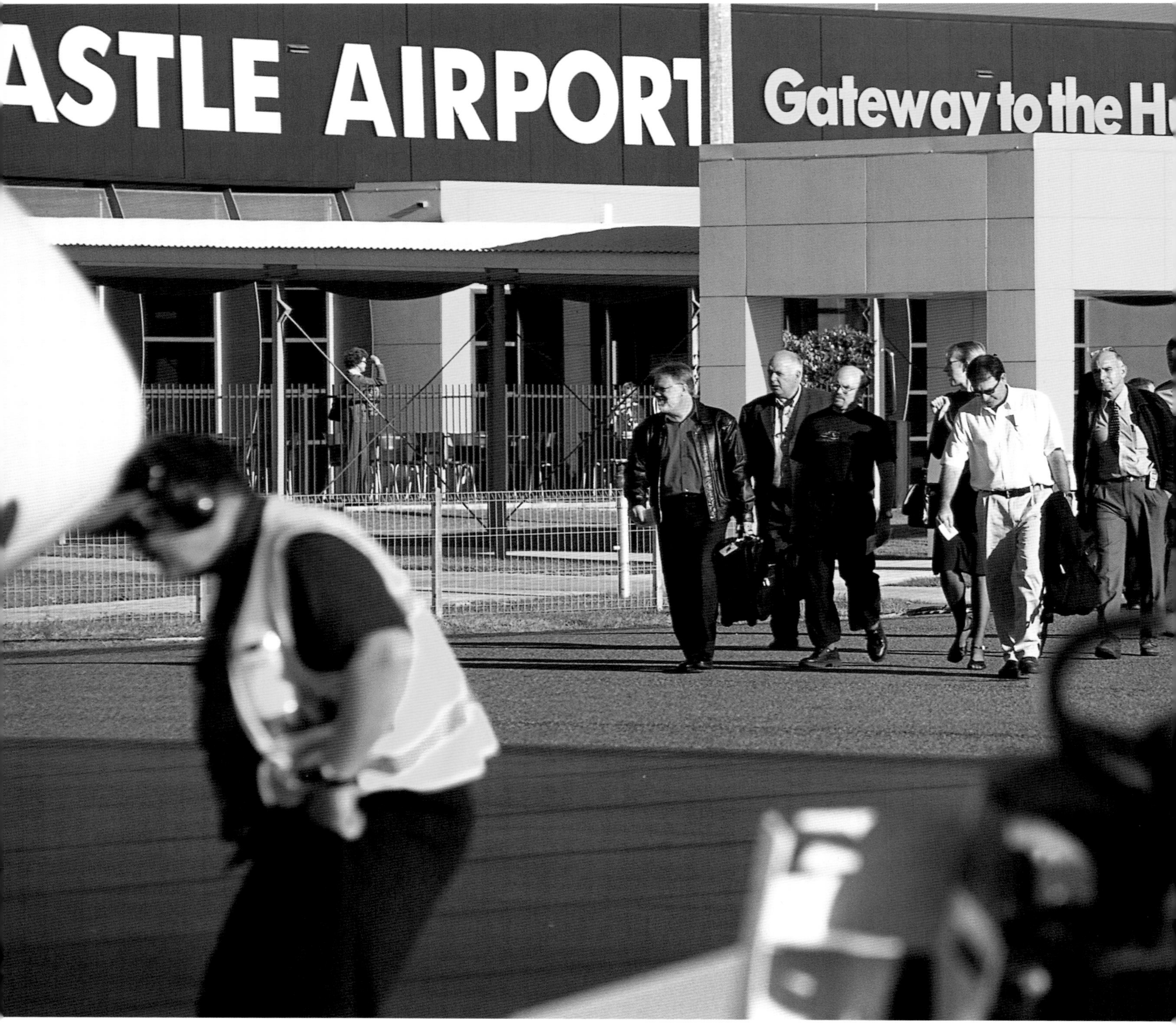
ASTLE AIRPORT
Gateway to the Hu

'Our very big world is becoming very small and as clever as we may be as individual companies we are relatively small. So it is through networking that we can become bigger than a single company.'

—Joss de lllius, Managing Director, Waratah Engineering

GRAINCORP OPERATIONS LTD

'GrainCorp delivers storage and logistics solutions for bulk grain export at its Newcastle terminal. Through dedication to our customers, by diversifying core business activities and embracing change, we will continue our strong contribution to Newcastle—well into the new century.'

—John Sneddon, GrainCorp Newcastle Terminal Manager

Above: Steve Matkovic, Grain Terminal Operator.

See page 175 for contact details >

'Take away the barriers and companies can fulfil their real potential. Ipera can deliver much more telecommunications capacity to business than traditional solutions at a fraction of the cost. That benefit can then be leveraged to provide innovative solutions to business problems ... and even more competitive advantage!'

—Chris Deere, Managing Director, Ipera Network Computing Pty Ltd

IPERA NETWORK COMPUTING PTY LTD

Ipera is a Newcastle company providing a broadband telecommunications network capable of delivering traditional and innovative new services to the region. Fast Internet access, low-cost telephony, networking and outsourced services previously thought to be outside the grasp of all but the biggest corporate players are now viable for small to medium enterprises.

With a strong and experienced team, Ipera is able to offer high-quality, reliable telecommunications, networking engineering and software development services, providing innovative and effective solutions which allow clients to focus on their core business.

The company's vision is to provide Hunter companies with the technology advantages and competitiveness of capital cities, by making leading edge IT and telecommunications solutions easy, accessible and cost effective.

'Take away the barriers and companies can fulfil their real potential. Ipera can deliver much more telecommunications capacity to business than traditional solutions at a fraction of the cost. That benefit can then be leveraged to provide innovative solutions to business problems ... and even more competitive advantage!,' says managing director Chris Deere.

See page 177 for contact details >

four
TRADITIONAL STRENGTH

Newcastle retains its industrial heritage but change is on the rise. Traditional industries are making the most of the region's natural resources with government support for environmentally friendly technologies.

Steel

Despite the calculated quest for change that has gripped Newcastle's civic, business and union leaders, care has been taken not to ignore the contribution made by the region's traditional industries. Steel may no longer dominate the employment market, but heavy industry retains its place in the Hunter's economic armory.

Under the name of OneSteel, much of the former BHP infrastructure lives on. BHP closed the Newcastle blast furnaces in 1999, but the downstream rolling mills that were grouped with the tubemakers business remain in operation.

OneSteel feeds its Newcastle mills from the company's Whyalla steelworks in South Australia, supporting a workforce of more than 2,000 in its various Hunter Valley divisions.

'We are creating an environment in Newcastle so that people can invest in the region with confidence and we will keep working on that.'

—Councillor John S Tate, Lord Mayor, The City of Newcastle

At Waratah, a few kilometres inland from the BHP site, stands the Comsteel operation owned by BHP's most recent competitor in the Australian steel industry, the Victorian-based Smorgon group. The Waratah plant is based around an electric arc furnace, recently upgraded at a cost of about $15 million. It produces a range of specialty forging steels, construction steels, merchant bars and grinding media.

A loyal and efficient workforce of about 640 produces about 280,000 tonnes of steel each year. The recent overhaul saw a number environmental improvements that has given the plant a longer than expected life span.

Aware of the importance of a continued, productive steel industry, the New South Wales (NSW) government has encouraged new players to set up in Newcastle and a new generation of steel plants—using cleaner, quieter, more efficient technologies—are set to be built in the Hunter region over the coming years.

Most prominent of these is the Austeel plant proposed by an international consortium headed by Clive Palmer. Austeel's plans include a $5 billion, transnational venture to refine iron ore into hot briquetted iron (HBI) in Western Australia's Kimberly region. This will be shipped to Newcastle to be turned into steel in a state-of-the-art electric arc furnace steel making plant. The steel, in turn, would be marketed by South African-based trading company Macsteel International. Some of the world's great industrial companies, including Danieli, Lurgi and Corus are partners in the Austeel project.

The NSW government has pledged to support the project and has offered assistance to the value of $240 million in the form of tax breaks and infrastructure work on the Port of Newcastle with another $14 million pledged toward electricity costs.

OneSteel complex viewed from Kooragang Island.

progress

Protech Steel Pty Ltd has made great progress on plans for a $1.5 billion steel making and processing plant. Protech is working with a number of Australian and international companies on its ambitious plans.

The first stage of the Protech plant is a rolling mill, designed to process steel obtained from other manufacturers and turn it into various flat steel and plate products. The second stage is an electric arc furnace, which would be capable of producing about one million tonnes of steel annually and push the Protech workforce up to as many as 700.

Flat steels are high-value products, and the Protech mill would be in competition with Australia's biggest steelworks at Port Kembla. The NSW government has worked closely with Protech and has pledged assistance including the use of 75 hectares of industrial land on the southern side of Kooragang Island, looking across the Hunter River channel to the former BHP works.

Another steel plant has been proposed by Hunter Specialty Steels Ltd, a joint venture between Australian companies Boulder Steel Ltd and Australian Overseas Resources Ltd.

The $780 million project is planned for a new industrial zone developed by Macquarie Generation around the Liddell and Bayswater power stations, located south-east of Muswellbrook. Construction on the 100-hectare site is set to begin in the first quarter of 2002. The plant's production target is 260,000 tonnes a year of stainless steel and other specialty products for the construction, automotive and aircraft industries.

The new industrial zone will also be home to a $95 million sodium chlorate plant to be located on an eight-hectare site near the Bayswater Power Station. The plant is being built by a subsidiary of US company Sterling Chemicals and will have a production target of 60,000 tonnes a year.

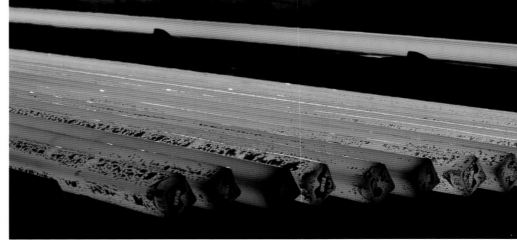

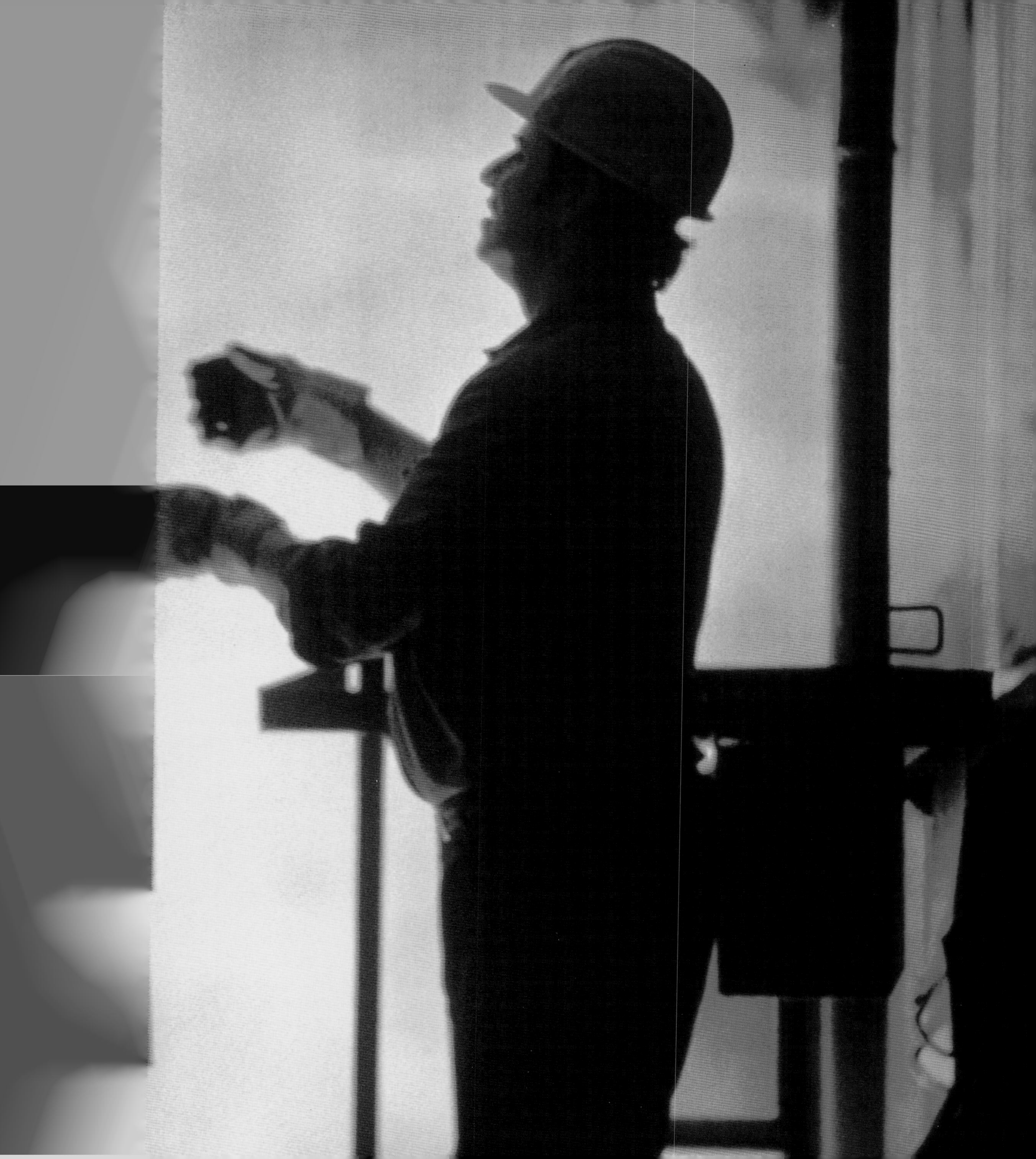

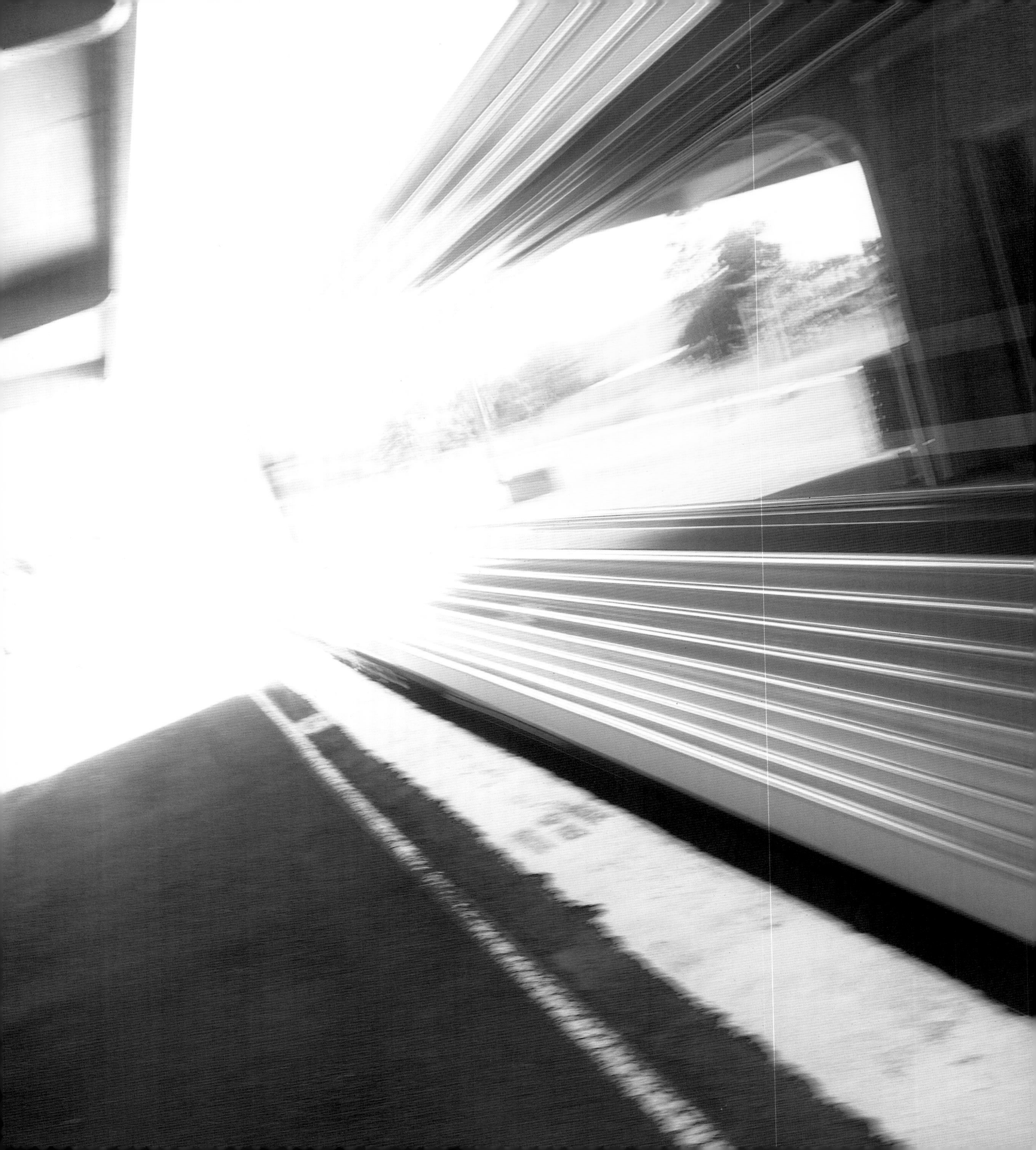

One of Newcastle's most venerable engineering institutions, A Goninan and Co, entered a new phase in August, 1999, when its former owners, Howard Smith Pty Ltd, sold it to the diversified industrial company United Group. The sale ended a 35-year relationship between Howard Smith and Goninan, which had grown from a Newcastle factory to become a national operation with strategic links into South-East Asia. It also saw Goninan's international technology partner, General Electric, take a 14 per cent stake in the United Group, emphasising its confidence in Goninan's long-term future.

Throughout the 1980s and early 1990s the sprawling Broadmeadow workshops were a hive of activity as a workforce of up to 600 designed and built Sydney's Tangara trains for the NSW government. United Goninan's most recent major Australian rail contract is for high-speed diesel trains bound for Western Australia.

United Goninan's export credentials were cemented in the late 1990s when hard work in South-East Asia paid off with two light rail refurbishment contracts in the highly competitive Hong Kong market.

In March 2001, the NSW government announced it would spend $50 million for seven new diesel trains to run between Newcastle and Maitland. United Goninan and Clyde are front-runners for this contract.

When Clyde Engineering won a 1998 contract to design and build a new fleet of passenger cars for the Sydney rail system, it gave a new lease of life to the former State Rail workshops at Cardiff. More than $9 million was spent refurbishing the workshops. Now, a crew of about 170 employees, including 20 apprentices, is turning out a total of 81 double-decker rail cars. Various parts of the contract are being built at other Clyde facilities around Australia, but most of the construction, and a 15-year maintenance contract, is being carried out at Cardiff.

The first stage of the contract is worth $300 million, and the NSW government has indicated it is considering ordering a second fleet of the Millennium train. The Millennium trains will run in units of four carriages and are designed to replace the last of Sydney's 1960s Tulloch carriages. The new trains will be quiet and air-conditioned, and include video surveillance cameras for greater passenger security.

coal

Coal has always been important in Australia and after 200 years of development the Australian coal industry is the most advanced and efficient in the world. Australia is the world's biggest coal exporter and black coal is its most lucrative export product; earnings have topped $12 billion annually in recent years. Hunter Valley coalfields are responsible for nearly $5 billion of this total and the Port of Newcastle is the world's biggest coal-loading port, rivalled only by Richards Bay, South Africa.

In recent years the NSW coal industry has produced more than 100 million tonnes of coal annually, about 80 per cent of which comes from the Upper Hunter Valley coalfields of Newcastle, Singleton and Gunnedah. These fields provide most of Australia's lower-energy coals—steaming or thermal coals—for power stations.

In the past decade, the Australian coal industry has undergone a number of changes that have resulted in productivity improvements and lower production costs. This has allowed the industry to keep pace with the slow but steady decline in the price of globally traded coal.

The coming decade is likely to see more changes in terms of both growth and rationalisation. Already, there has been a concentration of ownership in the industry with three companies— Rio Tinto, Glencore and Coal Operations Australia Limited—dominating production. NSW government research suggests that nearly half of the Port of Newcastle's coal exports will come from new and expanded open-cut mines in the Upper Hunter Valley.

Port Waratah Coal Services (PWCS) is one company that is leading the industry's growth. Since 1994, the company has spent approximately $700 million on expansions at its Kooragang Island coal terminal and,

Coal reclaimer on Kooragang Island, home to Port Waratah Coal Services terminal.

together with its older terminal at Carrington, increased its capacity to 89 million tonnes. PWCS also plays another important role in its cooperation with coal companies, railways and road hauliers, and shipping companies to ensure that coal supplies run smoothly regardless of weather or other disruptions.

Hunter Valley mines are also leading the way on the environmental front with mine site rehabilitation and revegetation schemes. Native forests are being re-established on previously cleared areas, while a salinity trading agreement for water discharges has improved water quality along the Hunter River.

Hunter Valley coalfields account for $5 billion of Australia's annual coal export total and the Port of Newcastle is the world's biggest coal-loading port.

Long before BHP began building the steelworks, a colonial offshoot of a British firm, the Sulphide Corporation, chose a then isolated lakeside spot, Boolaroo, to build a zinc and lead smelter. It was 1897 and the plant has been in continuous production since.

Pasminco took over the plant in 1988 and an extensive environmental spending program has dramatically reduced airborne and fugitive emissions. The company has bought a number of houses to form a buffer zone around the smelter and a complex system of monitors keep an accurate eye on the smelter's performance. Pasminco is an important employer in the region, employing about 640 people, producing about 64,000 tonnes a year of zinc and 35,000 tonnes of lead.

With smelters at Kurri Kurri and Tomago, the Hunter region produces about 600,000 tonnes of aluminium a year, or about one-third of Australia's overall production.

The Kurri Kurri operation, established in 1969, has endured the pressures endemic in mature businesses worldwide. After a decade of business restructuring and industrial relations improvements, it has emerged a stronger, leaner business. Its long-term future was secured following the $490 million purchase by German company VAW Aluminium AG in mid-2000. The Kurri Kurri smelter is the largest single employer in the Cessnock region with nearly 600 employees.

The Tomago Aluminium smelter is seen as one of the region's landmark industrial facilities. It was built between 1981 and 1983 under an innovative industrial relations framework that set the agenda for much wider industrial reform. The Tomago smelter was founded by French aluminium company Pechiney, CSR (Gove Aluminium), AMP Society, VAW Aluminium AG and Hunter Douglas, which is no longer involved.

The first expansion at Tomago began in 1991 with a third potline, which began production in 1993. Further expansions took place in 1997–98 with the extension of its original potlines. The smelter currently produces about 440,000 tonnes annually and there are plans to increase production to 600,000 tonnes if a fourth potline is built.

Tomago is also home to the 14-hectare industrial site of the Varley Group, a diversified engineering group employing more than 200 people. The group was founded in 1886 as a plumbing and boilermaking business, but its interests have matured to include general manufacturing, power, industry maintenance, ship repairs, defence and vehicles.

Varley Specialised Vehicles has become one of the group's biggest earners. It has received a federal government grant of $875,000 to back its fire-fighting vehicle project for the

supply of vehicles to NSW and Queensland city and country fire brigades. Jeff Phillips, Varley managing director, estimates the contract for NSW could be worth $100 million, while the Queensland contract would be around $20 million, representing a major boon for the Hunter region.

Defence is another major growth area for the group. Varley currently supplies products—logistics shelters, aircraft simulator cockpits and transportation containers—to three arms of the Australian Defence Forces. 'We've grown substantially in the past decade ... most of our work now comes from outside of the region and our customers come back to us because we get the job done with quality, service and [competitive] pricing,' Jeff Phillips says.

Right: The Forgacs floating dock facilities are crucial to the navy's maintenance and repair capabilities.

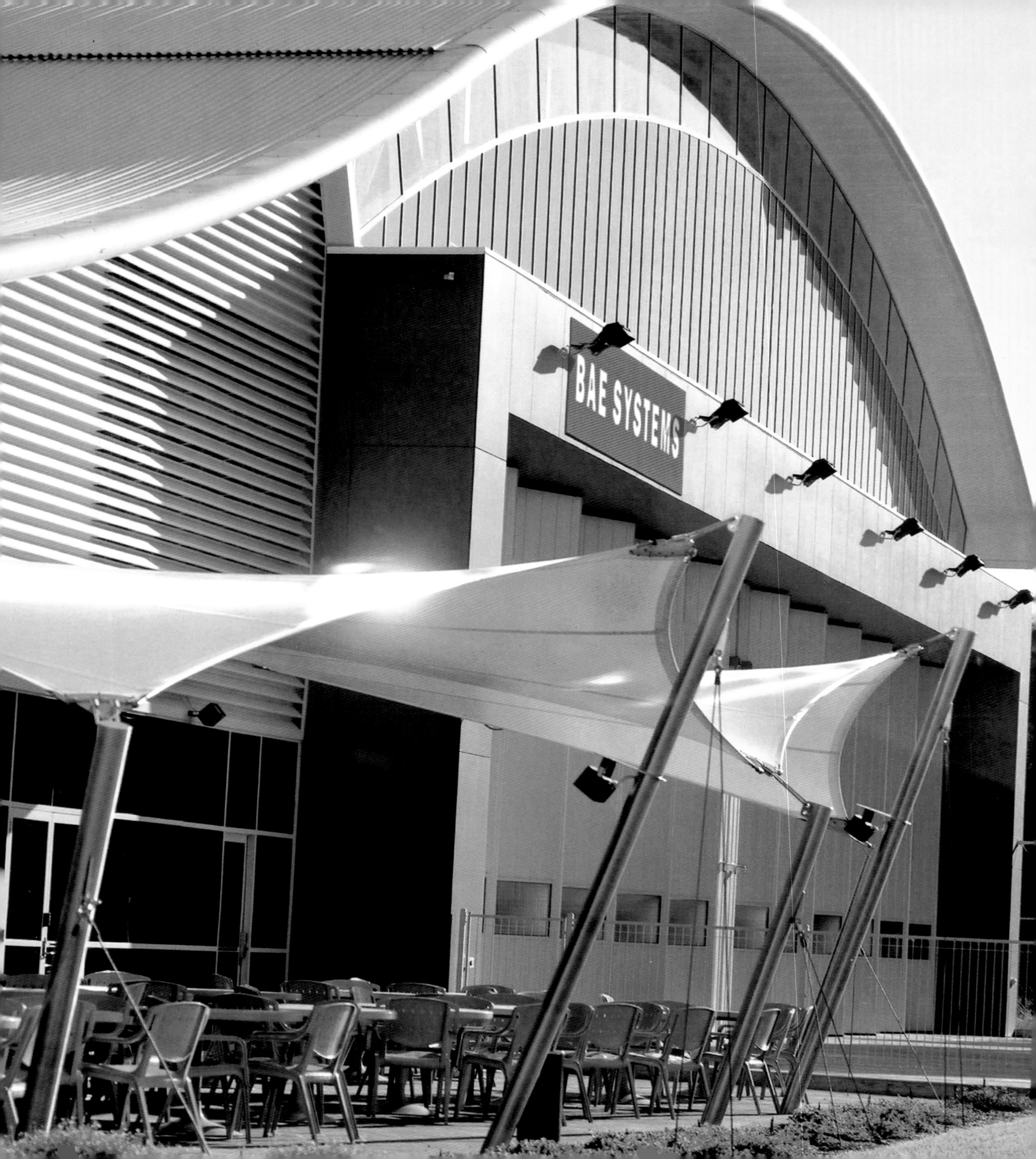
BAE SYSTEMS

defence

The Hunter Valley has a long history as the heartland of the defence industry in Australia and is home to major army and air force facilities. Hunter Valley industries have worked closely with defence departments and prime examples of their successful collaboration are the ADI minehunter facility at Carrington and the BAE SYSTEMS (formerly British Aerospace) assembly and maintenance hangar at Williamtown.

The RAAF base is one of Australia's biggest and busiest air defence operations. It boasts a runway capable of handling the world's largest domestic and military aircraft, servicing both the RAAF and Newcastle Airport. The base employs 2,100 service personnel and 300 civilians.

The civilian airport, a modern regional facility owned jointly by Newcastle City Council and Port Stephens Council, handles more than 200,000 passengers a year and provides a range of services to various destinations across the eastern states of Australia.

The board of Newcastle Airport has worked hard to develop a modern industrial base at Williamtown, and the BAE SYSTEMS facility has attracted new businesses to the site.

Newcastle has a long and proud record of building and maintaining ships for the navy, first through the State Dockyard on Dyke Point and then through the privately owned Carrington Slipways at Tomago. Facilities led by the Forgacs floating dock 'Muloobinba' are crucial to the navy's maintenance and repair capabilities. The Forgacs facility rivals the capacity of other Australian shipyards and should continue to participate in future naval shipbuilding projects.

Newcastle engineering firms did a substantial amount of fabrication work on the ANZAC Frigate project won by the Victorian-based consortium based around Transfield, but Newcastle's biggest modern naval shipbuilding contract has been the $1 billion Huon class minehunter fleet, being built at Carrington by ADI.

A workforce that peaked at about 500 has been engaged on the contract since 1998 and the final vessel is due for delivery in 2003. Vessel after vessel in the six-ship fleet has been launched on budget and on time. All up, an estimated 850 Hunter firms will earn more than $250 million from the seven-year project.

BAE SYSTEMS has an $850 million contract with the RAAF to assemble and maintain 33 Hawk Lead-in Fighter jets to replace the RAAF's ageing Macchi trainers. BAE SYSTEMS is working with more than 40 Australian companies including HUNTER Aerospace, Airflite and Qantas.

BAE SYSTEMS facility at Williamtown has lured new business to the site.

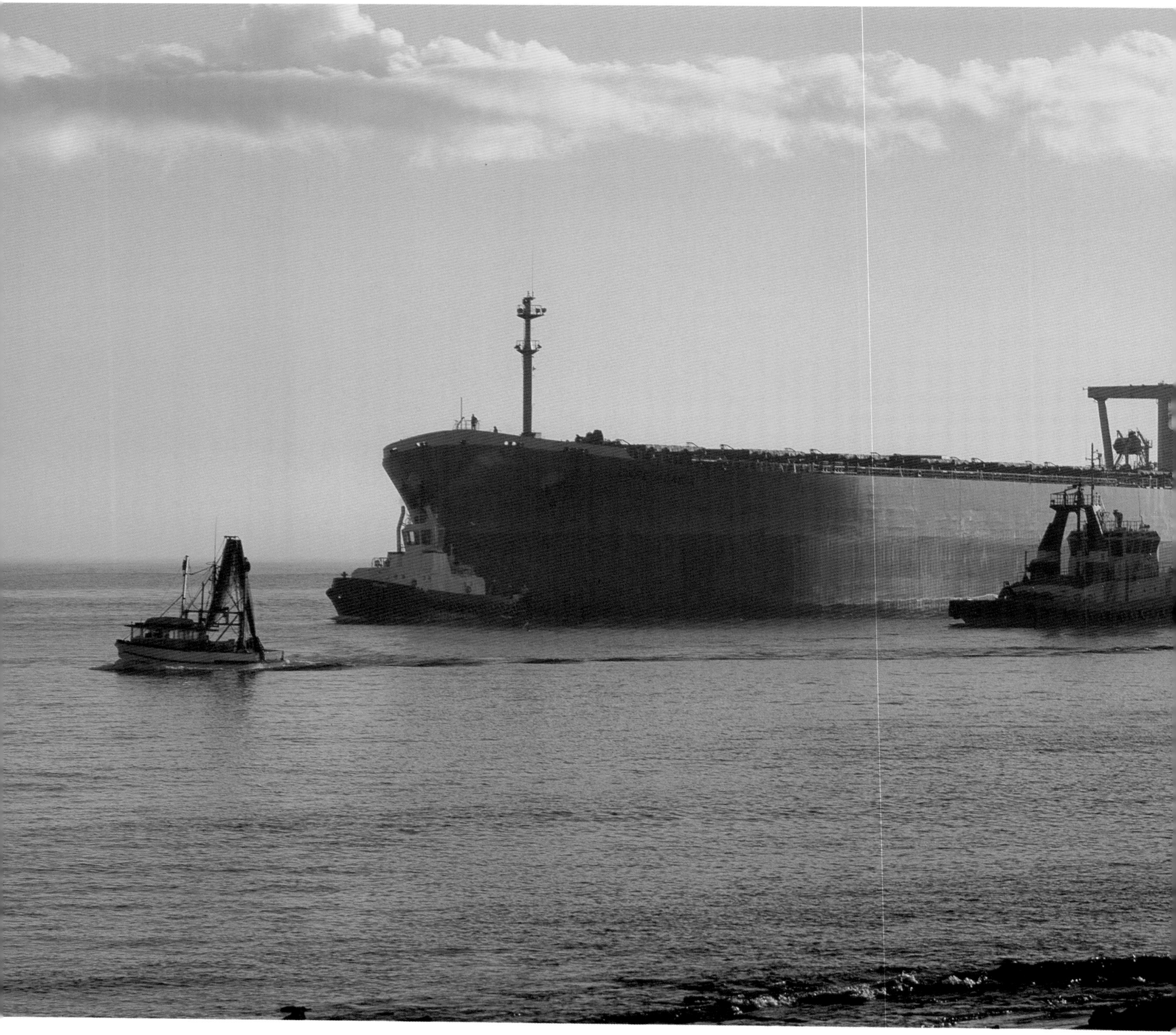

The Port of Newcastle is
the largest tonnage throughput port
in New South Wales and has more
than 3,000 shipping movements a year.
State-of-the-art navigation aids and
channel markers are used to ensure
the safe and efficient movement of
vessels through the port.

'Although Marathon Tyres is now considering international opportunities, our commitment to the Hunter region remains as strong as ever. With strong partnerships, the right people and a passion to do the job right, Newcastle is a great place to start and build a successful business.'

—Mike Nesbitt, Chairman, Marathon Tyres Pty Ltd

MARATHON TYRES PTY LTD

Keeping Business on the Road

It is a business cliché that the real action is not in the boardroom, but at the coalface, or 'where the rubber meets the road'. Marathon Tyres is proof that keeping the rubber on the road is a sure-fire formula for success.

Founded in the Hunter by Mike Nesbitt in 1970, Marathon Tyres has grown to become one of the major suppliers of tyres and related services in the mining and transport industries, with facilities around Australia, from Townsville to Kalgoorlie, Darwin to Melbourne. Asked for the secret to Marathon's success, Nesbitt is quick to answer. 'Partnerships, the best people and passion.'

Strong working partnerships with clients presented Marathon Tyres with the first opportunities for expansion. As the coal mining boom of the 1970s spread throughout the Hunter Valley, the company pioneered new

systems to help mining companies reap the maximum benefit from tyres for fleets of giant vehicles which can cost millions of dollars a year. Nesbitt says the Marathon philosophy of developing a partnership with clients is a key ingredient to maintaining and improving market share. 'Marathon people are often members of a mine's tyre management committee, sharing the responsibility of delivering the best result at the lowest cost.' Marathon's detailed knowledge and experience has also driven the production of tailor-made tyres for specific mine sites, with further improvements in productivity.

Determination to meet client needs has lead Marathon Tyres to develop a 'one stop' facility to provide all under-body services for trucks and buses. The Marathon objective is to deal with all aspects of the vehicle which affect tyre performance.

The second ingredient in Marathon's recipe for success is people. Nesbitt is proud that some of the employees now joining the company are the children of current employees. 'Our aim is that members of the team in years to come will ensure the Marathon story doesn't end, but keeps unfolding.' As well as retaining a wealth of industry knowledge, the multi-skilled Marathon employees are provided with a career path which ensures the company maintains the edge in experience on its competitors.

Passion for the business has also lead Marathon Tyres to develop new business opportunities which will drive the company's growth in the future. A flat tyre on a military or security vehicle, for example, can be a life-threatening event. Marathon has pioneered the use in Australia of new technology to maintain vehicle mobility.

Overcoming the challenges of globalisation also requires passion and commitment. Marathon has put years of effort into developing strong international connections to ensure its survival and success. Mike Nesbitt says experience means Marathon Tyres has the ability to recognise opportunities in niche markets when they arise. 'When we make a commitment to develop that opportunity we do it 110 per cent!'

See page 178 for contact details >

'For Robtec, helping the Hunter industry become more efficient and competitive is a source of great satisfaction. Our team of Sales and Support Engineers have experience in industry and mining and know how to deliver a solution that is going to work every time.'

—Rob Nichols, Founder and CEO, Robtec Control Solutions Pty Ltd

ROBTEC CONTROL SOLUTIONS PTY LTD

Innovation for Automation

In the global marketplace, the slightest competitive edge can make the difference. That's why the majority of innovative companies in the Hunter region trust Robtec to provide world-class devices and systems for control and automation of their plants.

Founder and Chief Executive Officer Rob Nichols launched the company in 1984, turning his engineering experience in a major resources company to solving control and automation problems for an ever-expanding list of clients in industry and resources. Robtec-installed systems can be seen in such varying environments as the massive Bengalla coal mine in the Upper Hunter Valley, the Port Waratah Coal Services coal loading facility in Newcastle Harbour, the Tomago Aluminium smelter and Nestlé production lines.

Robtec is a leading distributor for Rockwell Automation/Allen Bradley, but the most advanced technology is of little use if it isn't backed up by expert advice on applications and continuing support. Robtec has selected its team of sales and support engineers because of their extensive backgrounds in industry and mining, giving them a clear understanding of the challenges facing every client.

Whether the solution to the challenge is a simple electrical component, or a sophisticated plant and process control system, the quality of the advice and service is maintained at the highest level.

See page 184 for contact details >

'Control Synergy aims to break down the barrier between industrial control systems to provide true integration. Once the obstructions are removed the data flows smoothly, improving plant coordination and efficiency. That's the synergy … when all sections are meshed together, working towards a common goal.'

—Rob Nichols, Founder and CEO, Control Synergy Pty Ltd

CONTROL SYNERGY PTY LTD

Breaking Down the Barriers

The need to beak down communication barriers in control and automation systems led to the formation of Control Synergy. Calling on decades of experience with leading international control systems, Control Synergy set out to improve overall plant integration and efficiency.

Control Synergy offers a range of innovative technologies, including wireless data and inter-control system communications, pre-formed cable systems and electrical voltage surge protection systems. The technologies eliminate labour-intensive, repetitious work and help reduce equipment downtime.

This technology is being utilised at the Bengalla coal mine in the Upper Hunter Valley (right). Spread spectrum wireless technology enables high-speed collection of production and performance data.

See page 184 for contact details >

83

'For a major international company like Sandvik, a strong presence in the Hunter is important. The strength of the mining and metals industries in the region alone means Sandvik products and services are in high demand. The quality of those products and services makes Hunter industries more efficient and competitive.'

—David Macdonald, Sandvik Australia Pty Ltd

SANDVIK AUSTRALIA PTY LTD

Opposite, clockwise from top left: VA Eimco and Sandvik MGT specialises in products for mining of coal and other soft minerals; Sandvik's Mayfield plant, which manufactures cemented carbide products, is the largest of its kind in Australia; coil for sheets and plate is custom-cut to length; Sandvik Coromant is the world's leading manufacturer of cemented-carbide tools for turning, drilling and milling.

Specialising in Strength

As the fine product of another Hunter Valley vintage is prepared for bottling, the contribution of international company Sandvik may be difficult to ascertain. It's ever-present, however, as is the company's role in mining, manufacturing and engineering.

Sandvik has 35,000 employees in 130 countries around the world in three main divisions—Tooling, Mining and Construction, and Specialty Steels. The company first ventured into the Hunter in the 1960s, opening a small sales office, but demand for products and business opportunities has seen the Sandvik presence in the region grow dramatically.

Now Sandvik Australia makes a major contribution to the company's revenue, thanks in no small part to the success of the Hunter ventures.

For the burgeoning wine industry, the massive stainless steel tanks, which are part of every winery, are often constructed from high-quality Sandvik stainless steel. In a wide range of industrial operations across the nation, Sandvik steels are used where resistance to corrosion is paramount.

As the mining industry has grown across the region, so has demand for products for the mechanical excavation of both soft minerals and hard rock. At the business end of VA Eimco road headers and continuous miners (supplied by the Sandvik Mining and Construction Group from its Tomago headquarters), the picks and tools are also a Sandvik product, carefully machined and assembled at its Mayfield plant. Also produced at Mayfield are a wide range of cemented carbide products used in tooling across Australia and exported to Asia.

Sandvik Hard Materials is a world leader in cemented carbide blanks for tool manufacturers, components for the engineering industry and advanced cutting and forming tools. Cemented carbide products from the Mayfield plant are used in industries around the nation. The world's best practice standards are rigidly applied to the Hunter operation, making Sandvik customers more competitive on local and overseas markets.

The plant also manufactures some products for Sandvik Coromant, also a world leader in tools in cemented carbide, ceramics, cubic boron nitride and diamond for metalworking applications. The Hunter region's strong metal industries generate strong demands for Coromant's turning, milling and drilling systems, which contribute to process efficiency. Coromant also offers custom-made tool solutions.

See page 184 for contact details >

'In critical sectors such as defence, we have to provide solutions that are absolutely right the first time around. There is no margin for error. And the quality has to be of the highest order, because the next test will be under battle conditions and lives will depend on our products.'

—Jeff Phillips, Chairman and Managing Director, Varley Holdings Pty Ltd

VARLEY HOLDINGS PTY LTD

Success in the Challenge of Change

Defence. Aerospace. Power Generation. Transport. Just some of the industries serviced by the Varley team at the start of the 21st century. It is a list that can change rapidly, as the company is quick to respond to new directions and opportunities.

Founded towards the end of the 19th century, Varley has evolved to become a diversified engineering company, serving clients in the Hunter region, across Australia and overseas. Varley has worked with some of these clients for many years, and while the nature of their engineering problems may change, their faith in the solutions provided by Varley has not.

Asked to nominate the key factors in the company's success at meeting the challenge of change over the years, Chairman and Managing Director Jeff Phillips nominates three: a focus on customers, dedication to quality, and acceptance of change.

'The fact that we have retained customers for many, many years is testament to our belief that we can offer the best customer service through open and honest relationships,' says Phillips.

Because Varley is often asked to find solutions to clients' problems means that the relationship is far more than client and contractor. It's more like a partnership.

One example was the development of new vehicles to deliver and prepare explosives. The project not only met the client's demanding requirements ... it gave the Varley team new skills, which were put to use developing a new range of specialised vehicles, including urban and airport fire appliances.

'In our workshops we build these vehicles from the ground up. In an age of mass

Opposite, from top: Deployable missile tracking stations; main workshops, Tomago NSW; the world's most advanced Emergency Response Vehicles.

manufacture, clients come to us knowing that they will receive a unique solution to their needs, with no compromise.'

For a company to remain successful and a leader in general engineering for more than 100 years, the quality of work has to be of the highest order. That is why much of Varley's work is in the extremely demanding defence sector, with Army, Navy and Air Force, from projects such as the Hawk lead-in fighters for the RAAF, to the design and manufacture of military shelters and vehicles for the Army and advanced telemetry systems for the Navy.

The quality imperatives in defence work are crucial, says Phillips. 'That quality carries through from the ergonomics research, to the systems testing and the construction.'

The final quality which has been essential to Varley's success, says Phillips, is an acceptance of change. Phillips believes that this ability to adapt came from the varied nature of George Varley's original business. 'Because we can adapt to constantly changing social, environmental and technological standards—and see opportunities in those changes—we will continue to thrive. We are now looking forward to taking on competitors in a global marketplace.'

See page 188 for contact details >

NEWCASTLE : BUSINESS

In 1994, ADI and the Hunter 'teamed up' to win the Royal Australian Navy's Huon Class minehunter project. The Hunter enthusiastically supported ADI's bid and its goodwill toward ADI has never wavered. The highly successful project has duly rewarded the Hunter with local businesses winning contracts worth $300 million and providing 550 peak time jobs at ADI's Carrington site.

ADI LIMITED

ADI Limited is Australia's leading defence, systems and engineering company. ADI has an annual turnover of $600 million and a workforce of around 3,000. The company has a significant presence in the Hunter region through its minehunter ships project.

ADI provides its defence and commercial customers with a range of world class technology products and services including command information and communication systems; heavy engineering; marine engineering; ship building; ordnance and facilities management.

ADI is progressing in Sydney the $900m upgrade project for the Royal Australian Navy's six guided missile frigates while in Newcastle it is completing the production of the RAN's six state of the art Huon Class minehunter ships, a huge $1 billion contract.

The minehunter contract was awarded to ADI in 1994 after it had competed against many Australian and overseas companies. The project is a complex, high technology task, which has already won an engineering excellence award from the Institution of Engineers, Australia. At the project's peak, more than 500 highly skilled workers were employed at ADI's Newcastle harbour front site. The project is scheduled to end in 2003.

This successful project demonstrates not only ADI's capabilities but those of the many hundreds of Hunter region companies involved with ADI in producing the world's most advanced minehunters—on time and on budget.

See page 172 for contact details >

'Koppers Coal Tar Products is the legacy of our history of local investment in the Hunter region. We are a part of a thriving industrial community in Newcastle and our innovative use of resources is welcomed by other key employers such as aluminium smelters in the Lower Hunter.'

—Ernie Bryon, Managing Director, Koppers Coal Tar Products Pty Ltd

KOPPERS COAL TAR PRODUCTS PTY LTD

Preserving Local Industry

Established in Newcastle 1968, the Koppers Australia Group has been a part of the local business community for more than 30 years. Today it is the nation's largest manufacturer and exporter of coal tar by-products, wood preservatives and timber.

From supplies of carbon pitch for the Hunter's strong aluminium smelting industry to treated timber products like electricity poles, landscaping logs and rural fencing, Koppers maintains a standard of excellence to meet customer needs worldwide.

Koppers has a strong attachment to Newcastle with the Koppers Coal Tar Products division located at Mayfield. Originally located near the BHP steelworks, this division still enjoys the benefits of its access to rail and sea transport in and out of Newcastle.

Koppers is an example of the success many companies have found with their base in Newcastle—operating with complete autonomy while still benefiting from its international connections, particularly in marketing and technology.

This wealth of knowledge, together with local expertise and facilities, helps Koppers stay at the forefront of world technological advances in all areas of its operation. These are real benefits that reach its customers.

Koppers Australia also boasts its own successful operations overseas in countries including New Zealand, the Philippines, Malaysia, South Africa and the People's Republic of China.

See page 177 for contact details >

NEWCASTLE:BUSINESS

'OneSteel has strong historical links with Newcastle. Our strong market position is driven by our assets, our technology, our people and the strength and support of the community in Newcastle.'

—Geoff Plummer, President, Market Mills

ONESTEEL LIMITED

OneSteel Limited is the leading manufacturer of steel long products and leading distributor of metals in Australia. It has operations located Australia-wide and in New Zealand and North America. OneSteel operates as four main business units: Whyalla Steelworks; Market Mills; Distribution; and Steel and Tube Holdings in New Zealand. It employs 7,000 people with revenues of $3 billion per annum and is listed on the Australian Stock Exchange.

In the Hunter region, OneSteel has a significant presence through its Market Mills operations, which is headquartered in Newcastle. It manufacturers and supplies a comprehensive range of steel rod, bar, wire, wire rope, pipe, tube and structural steels. Market Mills' products are used primarily in the construction, rural, manufacturing and mining industries in Australia.

Market Mills produces 1.5 million tonnes of steel products annually and has an annual turnover of $1 billion. It is the largest private employer in the Newcastle region with approximately 2,000 employees and approximately $300 million is spent each year in the local community.

OneSteel's clear focus in Market Mills is on customers, world-class manufacturing and ongoing improvement through innovation and the involvement of our people.

See page 182 for contact details >

'Along with determination to achieve a high level of coal loading efficiency, PWCS combines dedication to quality and commitment to the environment and the safety of its employees, with recognition of its role in the Hunter community, PWCS will maintain this dedication and commitment as demand for Hunter coal continues to grow.'

—David Brewer, General Manager, Port Waratah Coal Services Ltd

PORT WARATAH COAL SERVICES LTD

From the Valley to the Sea

Coal holds a special place in the history of the port of Newcastle. Coal from the fledgling mines of the colony became the first export in 1797, pioneering an industry which would grow to become one of the biggest export coal terminals in the world. Using facilities at Carrington and on Kooragang Island, Port Waratah Coal Services Ltd (PWCS) is at the hub of this thriving export trade.

Each year, hundreds of ships arrive in the port, and leave for international markets, their holds laden with thermal and coking coal from mining operations dotted across the Hunter region.

Coordinating that complex coal chain, and ensuring it keeps rolling, requires a cooperative approach. PWCS links producers and marketers, rail and port organisations to ensure the product is soon on its way to customers throughout Asia and Europe.

Owned by coal producers and Japanese coal customers, the company is a unique example of cooperation. PWCS continues to show its high level of confidence in the future of the coal industry in the Hunter with ongoing investment to enhance export capability. This will ensure Hunter coal will continue to fulfil the potential first unearthed more than two centuries ago.

See page 183 for contact details >

'Tomago Aluminium is proud of its role as a major employer, exporter and revenue earner for the Hunter. We are continually looking at ways to increase the efficiency of our operations to competitively position the plant globally, attract further investment to the Hunter and secure the long-term future of the industry in this region.'

—Doug Parrish, Plant Manager, Tomago Aluminium Company Pty Limited

TOMAGO ALUMINIUM COMPANY PTY LIMITED

Tomago Aluminium produces high quality, value-added aluminium products for the export market using two key components—world's best technology and a highly skilled workforce.

The plant, situated 13 kilometres north west of Newcastle, employs 1,050 people and produces 447,500 tonnes of aluminium per year, making it one of the largest smelters in Australasia.

Competing globally in one of the world's most demanding international markets, where quality supply and continuous improvement are paramount and the competition is tough, Tomago Aluminium's results are testament to the region's industrial expertise.

As one of the region's largest employers, Tomago Aluminium represents a major economic investment in the Hunter, contributing to the creation of jobs and the enhancement of sustainability and diversity in the valuable manufacturing industry. The company earns more than $800 million per year in export revenue—a significant contribution to both the local and national economies.

Tomago Aluminium recognises the important role it has to play in the economic, social and cultural life of the community. Accordingly, the company is involved in many sponsorship programs and initiatives that provide opportunities for employees and families and which benefit the local community both directly and indirectly.

See page 187 for contact details >

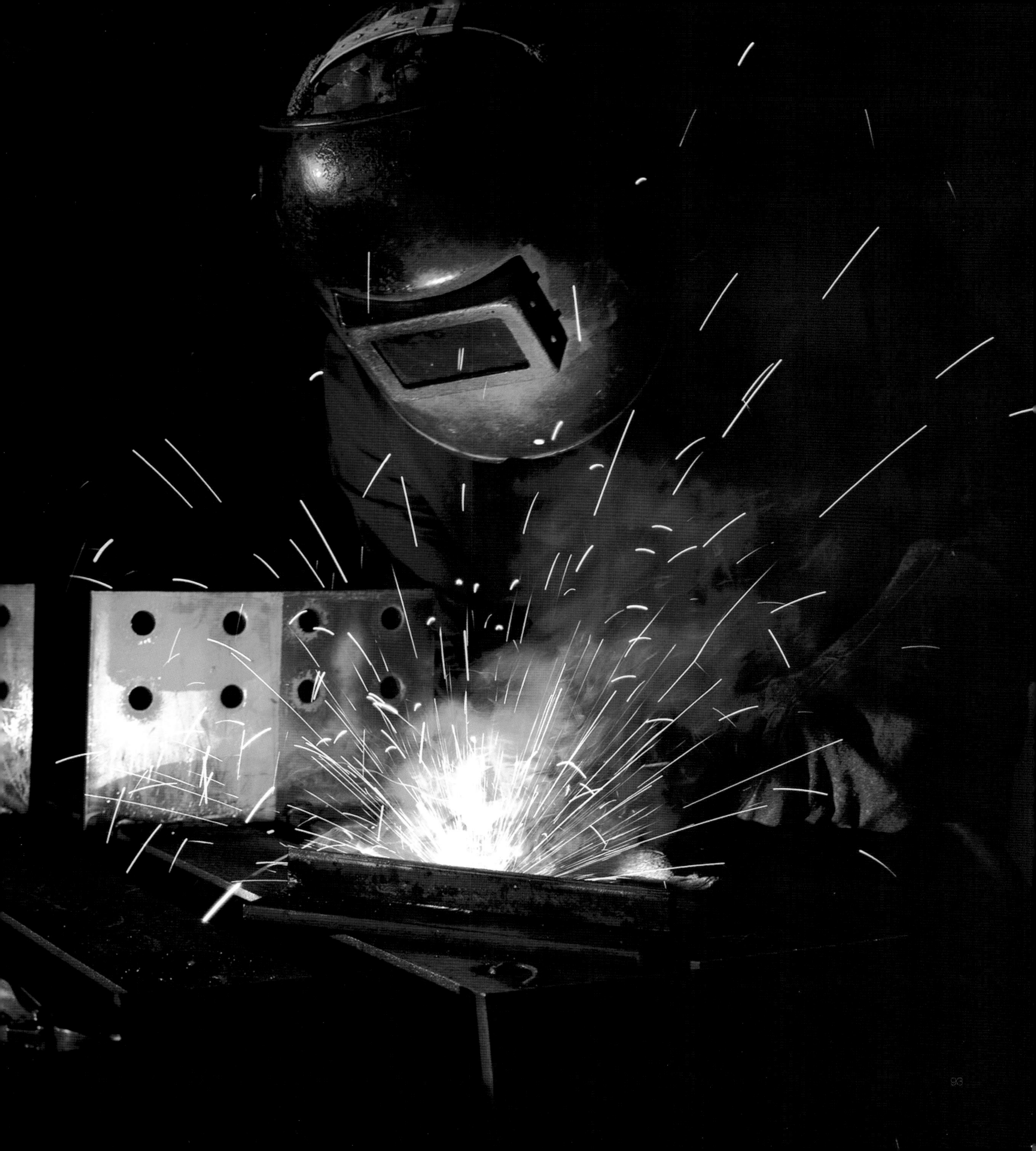

five
POWER

Newcastle and the Hunter Valley are key generators of power in New South Wales and are taking a leading role in energy sustainability.

The National Competition Policy has ushered in a rapidly changing new order. Some states have privatised their entire power generation sector, while others, such as New South Wales (NSW), have opted to keep the industry largely in public ownership, allowing competition from private sector generators and from energy companies in competing sectors such as gas. The Australian experience is being repeated around the world, as economic rationalism and global economics take effect.

Competition policy was introduced beginning with a series of steps in 1997 and full contestability for all power contracts scheduled for introduction by mid-2002. This should lead to

'There's a better understanding of the environment now ... I used to wonder if people in the street knew what we meant when we talked about sustainability ... I believed we needed to make the concept more relevant.'

—Councillor John S Tate, Lord Mayor, The City of Newcastle

substantial savings in power costs, especially for large and medium-sized businesses using considerable amounts of electricity. For generators and distributors it means competing on the open market for business that was once dictated purely by geography.

These changes offer a range of opportunities and challenges for Newcastle and the Hunter Valley, which account for nearly 90 per cent of NSW's electricity production in a series of coal-fired steam thermal power stations. These stations are managed by three state-owned corporations, Eraring Energy (Eraring power station), Macquarie Generation (Bayswater and Liddell) and Delta Electricity (Vales Point and Munmorah).

The Hunter Valley's power stations have steadily improved their thermal efficiencies (fuel to power ratios), from about 21 per cent in the 1950s to more than 35 per cent in the mid-1990s.

The growing efficiency of the network, combined with the international move to more energy efficient technologies and practices means the NSW government sees no need for major new generating capacity this decade. The Hunter Valley's power stations have also improved their environmental credentials, reducing dust and sulphur emissions substantially.

Two of the state's biggest electricity distributors, EnergyAustralia and Country Energy, are prominent in the Hunter

region. EnergyAustralia was created in 1996 by the merger of the Sydney-based Prospect County Council and the Newcastle-based EnergyAustralia. The smaller share of the market belongs to Country Energy, which was formed by the amalgamation of three regional NSW distributors, Advance Energy, Great Southern Energy and the Port Macquarie-based NorthPower.

NorthPower's geographical area had included the northern and western regions of the Hunter Valley. Aggressive marketing has seen it secure a number of high-profile customers in the early stages of contestable electricity.

Competition policy is leading to substantial savings in power costs, especially for large and mid-size businesses using considerable amounts of electricity.

A growing number of private energy generators are selling power into the NSW grid, and the privately owned and operated Redbank Power Station at Warkworth, near Singleton, is one of the most prominent.

The $320 million station is a revolutionary energy project using coal tailings, which are usually discarded, as its main fuel. Redbank's ability to use treated waste as fuel is a crucial development for the industry as disposal of coalmining tailings has been a major environmental challenge for Hunter Valley coalminers.

Redbank's technological breakthroughs include the Jameson Cell, developed by Newcastle academic Professor Graeme Jameson, and fluidised bed combustion, developed by ABB Power Generation Ltd. The Jameson Cell separates useful powdered coal from the liquid slurry of the tailings dam, while fluidised bed combustion allows powdered coal with its high ash and moisture contents to be burnt efficiently.

Redbank will produce about 130 megawatts of power—compared with the 2,640 megawatts of its neighbours Liddell and Bayswater—but the deregulated electricity market allows small generators to operate without disadvantage to the major power suppliers. The station has proved so successful that planning has begun on a second station at another Hunter mine.

Redbank generates about 75 per cent of its electricity from tailings at the nearby Warkworth coalmine, relying on normal 'run of mine' coal for the remaining 25 per cent of its energy needs. As such, it is a traditional fossil fuel power station designed with the increasingly important need to reduce greenhouse gas emissions in mind.

Together with competition policy, the greenhouse debate is the most important influence on the modern power industry and increasing amounts of research and development funds are

being dedicated to the search for cleaner and more effective energy.

This work falls into two categories. One group of projects, exemplified by Redbank, uses traditional furnace/boiler technology in new ways. The second comprises sustainable energy projects, using the sun, wind and water to generate electricity. The importance of both groups lies not in their actual power generation, which remains small, but in their development potential.

Surveys have shown domestic consumers are prepared to pay a substantial premium for power generated by renewable sources. The public expects cleaner, greener energy and in meeting the market EnergyAustralia and NorthPower have both developed niche green electricity products.

Green energy projects built or in development in the Hunter include:

- A biomass power station, burning waste timber from forests in the Upper Hunter, planned for Raymond Terrace, on Newcastle's northern boundary.
- A 600-kilowatt wind turbine built on Kooragang Island described as Australia's first modern large-scale wind turbine. Windmills are common sights in the UK and Europe, but their scarceness in Australia means the Kooragang turbine is a city landmark.

Right: Located on Kooragang Island, the EnergyAustralia windmill, one of the area's sustainable energy projects, is a city landmark.

power

One of the most obvious sources of power for electricity is the sun. Solar powered photovoltaic cells are in the experimental phase of development. Australian government research suggests that world production of solar panels in 1997 resulted in units capable of generating about 130 megawatts of power; 10 megawatts of the world total made is in Australia.

Production of solar panels is expected to double every three years and the solar power industry has moved from concentrating on remote area supplies and consumer products to integrated solar panels linked to mainstream power grids. Japan aims to have 4,600 megawatts of solar power in its grid by 2010, and the United States wants one million household solar power panels by the same time.

A solar farm at Singleton, operated by EnergyAustralia, is one of the 20 biggest of its type in the world, producing 500,000 kilowatts, or enough energy for 6,000 'pure energy' households. The Singleton farm prevents about 500 tonnes of greenhouse gases from atmospheric release each year, supporting the reduction of global warming.

The Hunter Valley has always been a key generator of electricity in NSW and it is now taking a leading role in the minimisation of power use. Newcastle is putting sustainability first and is being recognised for its efforts.

The United Nations' International Council for Local Environmental Initiatives

(ICLEI) recently voted Newcastle as one of the top three environmental cities in the world. A lot of the credit for that recognition goes to the Australian Municipal Energy Improvement Facility (AMEIF), a Newcastle City Council business unit charged with helping the city achieve its aim of becoming the South-East Asian centre for the sustainable energy industry.

AMEIF was formed in late 1998, but Newcastle council has been energy conscious since the mid 1990s. In 1995 the council's power bill topped $1 million. Five years later it was down to $650,000 with about one-third of those savings coming from cheaper power prices. The majority of the reduction came from energy saving practices and devices. The council approved a $400,000 'retrofit' of various lighting and other electrical devices, which paid for itself within two years.

Realising the opportunity for a new industry based on sustainability, the council voted to allocate its annual power bill savings to a revolving energy fund to buy products and services to further cut energy consumption and power costs. Many of AMEIF's energy-saving projects, such as retrofitting of low-energy lighting, are labour intensive, meaning the organisation is not only saving ratepayers money, it is creating work.

Based on the council's energy budget, AMEIF has calculated that an Australia-wide retrofit based on the nation's $12 billion annual power bill would generate more than 45,000 jobs for a year.

AMEIF is working with the Australian government and a range of key energy, water and waste agencies to form a Greenhouse Action Partnership (GAP) to provide the community with regular updates on actual greenhouse gas emissions caused by the city. This information will be promoted on a new council website, www.climatecam.com.

In a few short years of operation, AMEIF has become a national and world leader in its field. Backed by the Commonwealth's Australian Greenhouse Office, AMEIF has a contract to train 200 councils on energy saving initiatives. Many of these councils have in turn set up their own revolving energy funds.

The ICLEI commendation has given AMEIF an international profile, which was boosted recently when the organisation signed a memorandum of understanding to work on energy saving projects with Colorado's Rocky Mountains Institute, headed by 'natural capitalism' advocate Amory Lovins. When AMEIF invited him to visit Newcastle in July 2000, he was met by a packed house at two speaking engagements. His theory of 'natural capitalism' involves looking at the 'true cost' of all inputs into business, including energy and other natural resources.

AMEIF project director Peter Dormand says traditional fossil fuels are still likely to supply most of our energy needs for the foreseeable future. He believes that the most important thing is to reduce energy consumption by reducing demand.

The United Nations' International Council for Local Environmental Initiatives (ICLEI) recently voted Newcastle as one of the top three environmental cities in the world.

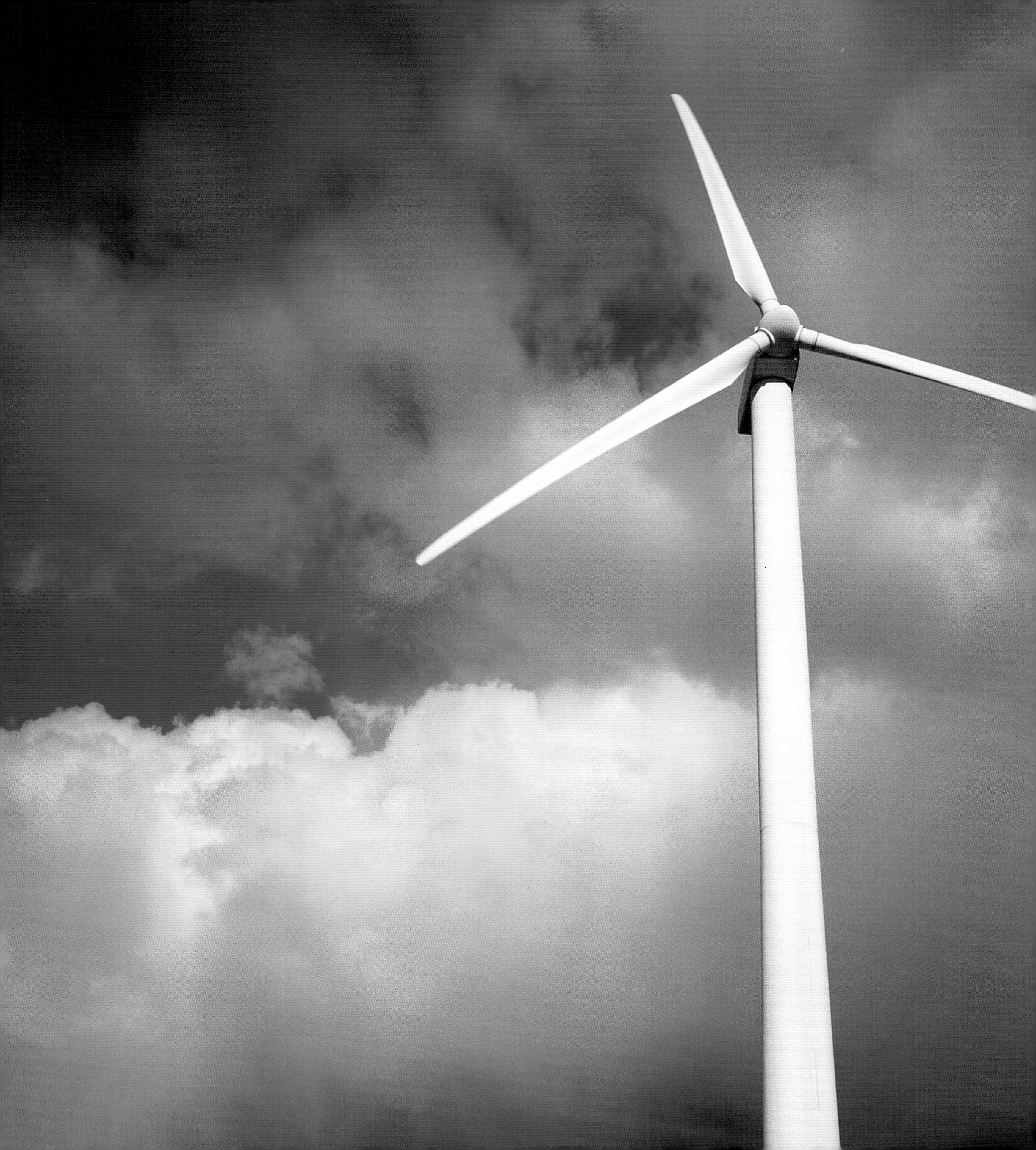

The Renewable Energy Projects Alliance
(REPA) is committed to developing
sustainable energy resources in
Newcastle and the Hunter region.
Projects such as the Kooragang Wind
Turbine and the Singleton Solar Farm
are evidence of the region's ongoing
commitment to the environment.

'EnergyAustralia is undertaking its biggest capital works program for decades to ensure Newcastle has first-class electricity infrastructure to support the region's growth. This will be a fundamental plank in ensuring the Hunter region can reach its potential and develop even further as a leading business and tourism centre.'

—Paul A Broad, Managing Director, EnergyAustralia

ENERGYAUSTRALIA

Providing energy for growth

First-class energy infrastructure is the cornerstone of any modern city. A safe and reliable electricity supply is becoming even more important as the Hunter region continues to embrace new technology-based industries to support its economic growth.

EnergyAustralia, which owns the region's electricity network, has provided a power supply for sustained business growth across the Hunter for many years. That is one of the reasons why Newcastle is delivering solid results for the nation's economy.

However, the pace of development; the way the growth is spreading out from traditional central business district areas due to a significant increase in industrial growth, small to medium enterprise businesses and export success for the region, means the electricity network needs to reach the next level.

The usual yearly growth in electricity is about 2–3% but in the EnergyAustralia market it is about 5%, and there are parts of the network in the Hunter where growth is reaching double figures.

As the region changes and positions itself as an integrated economy, the energy infrastructure must also change. A safe and reliable electricity network is absolutely fundamental to sustaining a competitive marketplace in the new world.

As a result, EnergyAustralia is undertaking its biggest capital works expansion in decades and is investing $250 million on new infrastructure in the next 10 years to keep pace with the Hunter's growth and build greater flexibility and redundancy into the network.

The first phase of this program will take place over the next four to five years, when EnergyAustralia will be spending more than

Right: Singleton Solar Farm. EnergyAustralia's 400 kW solar farm at Singleton is the largest solar power installation in the Southern Hemisphere and among the largest solar power stations in the world.

$180 million on boosting supply capacity and further raising operational standards. This is in addition to the $40 million spent each year on the existing network and $600 million spent supporting Hunter businesses.

As part of capital works planning, EnergyAustralia will be exploring alternatives to traditional engineering solutions to increase network capacity, like installing new substations and power lines.

Known as 'demand management', this explores ways of reducing the demand for power rather than building new infrastructure. By better managing this demand, it may be possible to delay some augmentation projects but still meet the community's demand for energy. Given EnergyAustralia has also entered the gas market, it has increased opportunities to deliver more environmentally friendly solutions to meeting energy growth.

A major contributor to the Hunter's sustaintable future is the relocation of the CSIRO's electro-technology centre to Steel River, which is not only a vote of confidence in the region's environmental credentials but a major opportunity for growth based on sustainable technologies.

As one of the country's leading energy companies, EnergyAustralia has the size and scale to invest in capital so that Newcastle has first-class energy infrastructure to underpin the business development strategies formulated by the Hunter's peak planning authorities and drive investment from new markets.

The company is committed to playing a leading role in delivering energy options that are sustainable and environmentally responsible and remains focused on ensuring the benefits gained from ongoing industry deregulation flow through to all business sectors.

See page 174 for contact details >

six
REACHING NEW MARKETS

Newcastle has always been a harbour city devoted to commerce and the port is on the cusp of a new age of growth.

A symbol of Newcastle's maritime heritage, and future, features prominently on the tip of Dyke Point, a peninsula in the centre of the harbour. Commissioned by the Newcastle Port Corporation as a bicentennial gift to the city, Destiny is a giant 9-metre bronze statue of a winged woman that greets every visiting vessel.

Newcastle has always been a harbour city and the harbour has always been dedicated to commerce. More than 1,500 cargo vessels visit the port each year and while coal continues to dominate Newcastle's export trade, the Newcastle Port Corporation recognises

'People associate the Hunter with steel and coal. However the real story is of a diverse population and regional economy with a wide range of enterprises using clever and innovative processes to produce international quality goods.'

—The Hon Richard Face, Minister Assisting the Premier on the Hunter

the need to diversify. Under the corporation's guidance, the port is on the cusp of a new age of growth.

The Newcastle Port Corporation—together with transport companies, stevedoring companies and terminal operators—has established a range of new berths, replacing ageing cranes and gantries with modern, efficient, cargo-handling infrastructure. Likewise, Newcastle City Council recognised the importance of retaining industrial land around the waterfront and put aside land within 750 metres of the high water mark for 'port-related' developments.

Nationwide waterfront reform has seen a massive increase in productivity on the Australian waterfront and Newcastle remains at the forefront of stevedoring efficiencies. Following trials begun in June 1999, Newcastle became the first commercial port in New South Wales (NSW) to use helicopter transfers for marine pilots. It still maintains the traditional method of ferrying the pilot to sea by small vessel when necessary.

In recent years a number of small 'boutique' cargo lines have begun operating in both directions. Numerous operators compete for business in

the port, and shipping, berthing and navigation charges remain extremely cost competitive and, in real terms, have fallen over the past five years.

To ensure the port can meet new levels of 21st century demand, the Port Corporation is planning a series of dredging programs to greatly increase its capacity.

The Port of Newcastle operates 24 hours a day with more than 3,000 shipping movements a year.

The Shortland Reach project is the first stage of the dredging programs and is upstream from the former steelworks and the Kooragang Island coal terminal. The dredging of this south arm of the Hunter River will open up industrial land on either side of the channel.

On the northern side, space will be created for another six berths. Other projects planned for this side of the river include the Protech steel plant, Robert Taylor's Austrack coal terminal and a berth for the Austeel steel plant.

On the southern side of the channel, large vessel access will be ensured beyond the proposed steelworks site HubPort container terminal to the Steel River industrial park. The channel deepening will end with a new swinging basin allowing vessels to turn around for their return journey.

The second stage of the dredging program is to be carried out in the existing harbour 'steelworks' channel. It will widen the channel to allow vessels to pass in opposite directions and deepen the channel at least another metre, allowing coal ships to load to a depth of 16.5 metres, effectively adding a potential 10,000 tonnes to each export coal cargo.

This is a strategic move considering that a number of important European subsidies for coal producers are scheduled to end in the coming years. The Hunter Valley's coal industry can expect to be a major beneficiary of the extra demand unlocked for non-European suppliers.

One of the most prominent businesses on Kooragang Island is Port Waratah Coal Services (PWCS), which operates the Port of Newcastle's two coal loaders. The PWCS offices are on Kooragang, along with the modern, and still growing, Kooragang Coal Terminal (KCT). The older and smaller of the two terminals, Port Waratah Coal Terminal, is located at Port Waratah, immediately downstream from the steelworks.

German construction company Bechtel has been overseeing a $345 million expansion project at Kooragang known as 'Stage III'. When the work is finished, PWCS will have an annual capacity of 89 million tonnes a year. Recent annual coal exports have totalled about 70 million and careful planning will see the Port maintain sufficient surplus capacity to ensure quick, efficient loading.

Ownership of both of Newcastle's coal loaders means PWCS has a monopoly in the industry, but because its management is focused on the needs of its coal company customers, coal loading charges are now far lower in real terms than at any time in the past.

As a mature resource, coal faces a long-term trend of gradually falling world

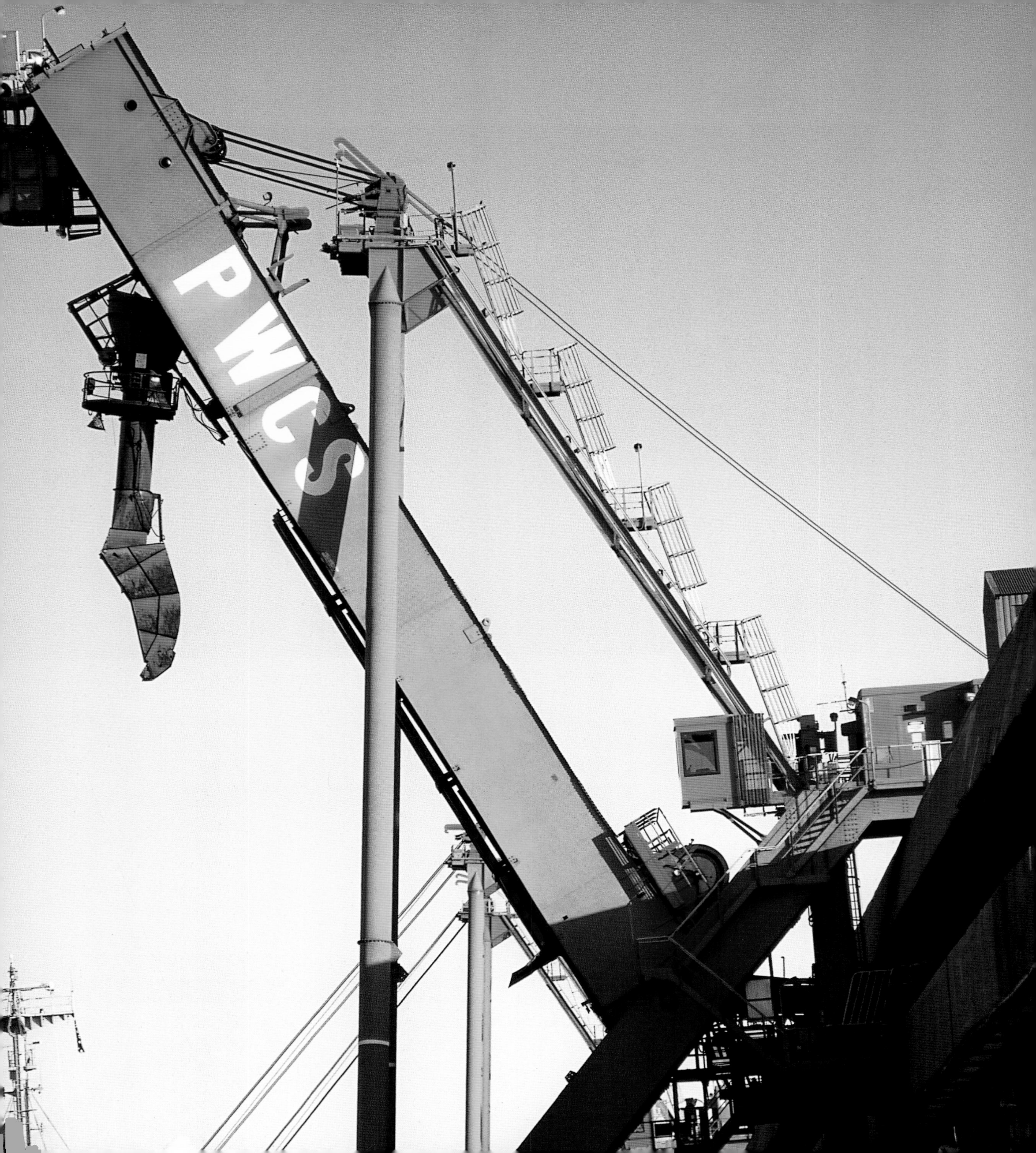
PWCS

Newcastle is trying to increase import cargoes and the HubPort project will give the city the competitive edge it needs to succeed.

prices, meaning coal companies need to trim their costs in order to remain competitive. Loading and transport are two areas where costs can be minimised and to this end a number of companies are exploring the possibility of a third Newcastle coal terminal.

The most high profile of these is the Austrack project, which would be located upstream of the PWCS operation at Kooragang Island. Austrack's founder, Sydney businessman Robert Taylor, spent more than a decade on the project and he is confident international

backers will see the plan come to fruition.

Newcastle's quest to increase import cargoes has not been an easy one. The multi-purpose shipping terminal (MPT), HubPort, was announced by BHP prior to its decision to withdraw from steel making in the region. The project is being developed by BHP and the Newcastle Port Corporation, although BHP intends to sell its stake in the project once remediation and construction work is finished and an operator is installed. Already, 19 companies from around the world

have registered expressions of interest to operate the facility.

With a nominal value of more than $270 million, HubPort is a project of national significance and is undoubtedly the key to a new era of prosperity. HubPort is expected to create jobs for about 350 people and support indirect employment of another 3,000.

The corporation's chairman, Wilton Ainsworth, says the project is the organisation's biggest challenge. 'If this project succeeds it will provide importers and exporters with a viable, cost-effective

and efficient alternative to capital city ports on the east coast of Australia.'

Newcastle business leaders believe HubPort's greenfield status and Newcastle's excellent intercity transport links will give its eventual customers a substantial natural advantage.

'Research shows us that it will be quicker to rail or even road haul containers from Newcastle to the western or northern suburbs of Sydney. With support from the state government, we believe HubPort can become the centre for container movement on the entire east coast.'

—Paul Murphy, Spokesman for the Newcastle and Hunter Business Chamber

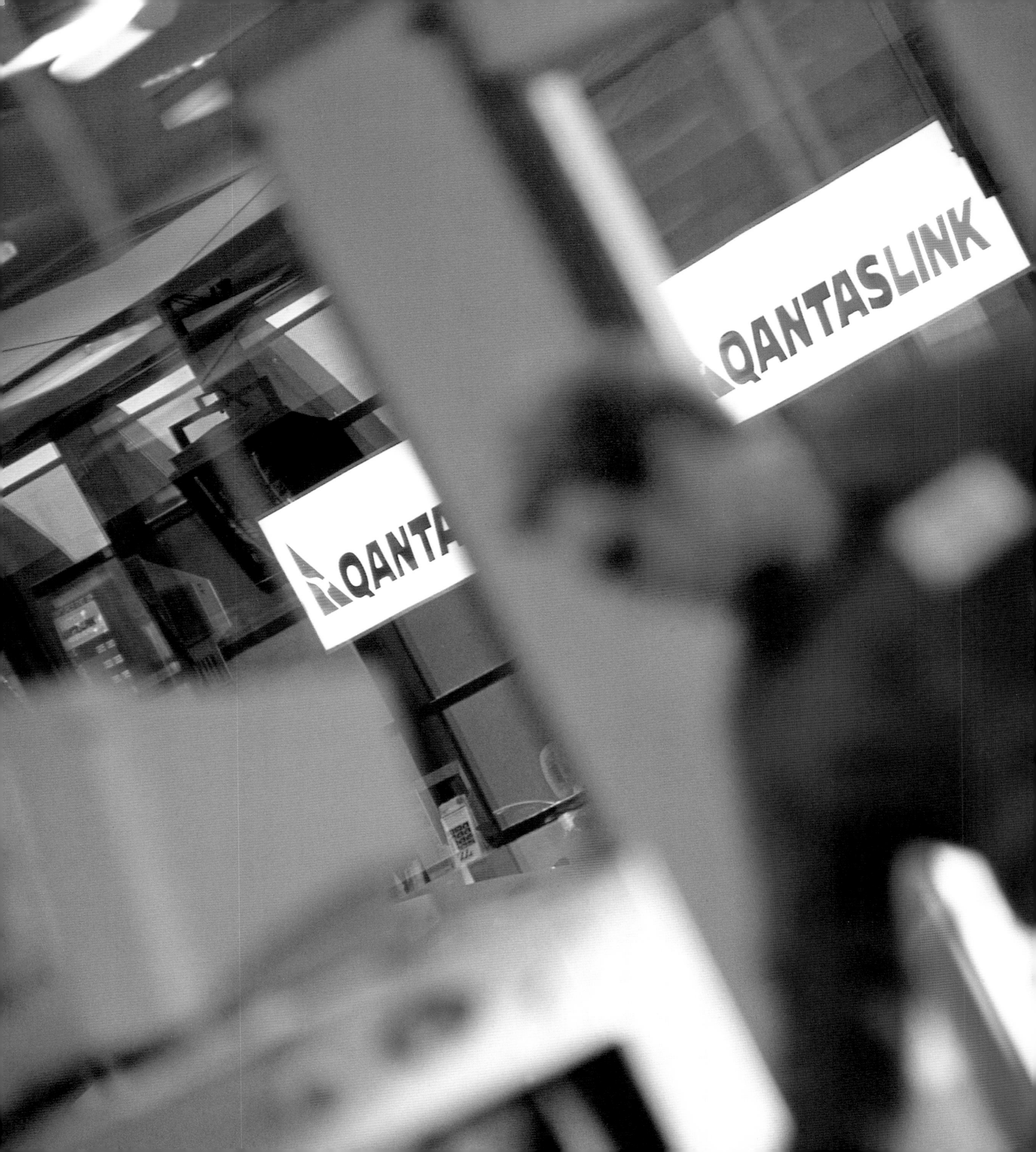
QANTASLINK
QANTAS

air links

Newcastle Airport is another key to the Hunter Valley's reach for new markets. Newcastle Airport's former chief executive, Sandy White, believes the airport's future lies in its ability to expand into a major regional operation.

One of its latest ventures is a push to establish regular direct flights between Newcastle and Auckland. The Sydney-based Centre for Asia Pacific Aviation believes there is significant untapped demand for direct air services between Newcastle and New Zealand.

Air services were liberalised between Australia and New Zealand in 1996, but until now, most of the growth has been on the New Zealand side. An estimated 500 people a week already travel from Newcastle to New Zealand without a direct flight, and it is believed that a Newcastle service would encourage more tourist travel.

'We've begun some small-scale international flights, such as a recent venture between here and Wellington, in New Zealand, and I see us tapping into a growing international charter tourism market,' Sandy White says.

'The international airport is off the political agenda for the time being and we're simply determined to keep on doing what we do well: provide a series of quick, efficient services to an increasing number of destinations.'

'The Hunter continues to produce almost a third of [New South Wales] exports, even though it is home to less than 10 per cent of the state's population.'
—The Hon Bob Carr, New South Wales Premier and Minister for the Arts

Newcastle Airport is a key in making the city a regional commercial hub.

NEWCASTLE:BUSINESS

NEWCASTLE AIRPORT LIMITED

'Newcastle Airport prides itself on linking the Hunter to Australia and the rest of the world. It makes a substantial contribution to the regional economy by establishing client partnerships, identifying customer and market opportunities, making provisions which exceed customer expectations and actively promoting the Airport as the aviation gateway to this magnificent region.'

—Air Vice Marshal Richard J Bomball AO AFC (retired), Chairman, Newcastle Airport Limited

Taking Flight

Busy executives around the world are familiar with the routine of checking in for flights upwards of half an hour before their departure. It is a waste of their valuable time but a necessary evil at the majority of airports. At Newcastle Airport, however, check in can be completed in a matter of minutes before departure. That is a factor which continues to drive the growth of business travel at one of Australia's fastest growing regional airports.

The arrival of new airlines and jet aircraft services has driven exponential increases in passengers, mainly from the corporate world. Direct flights to key destinations up and down the eastern seaboard allow business travellers to avoid congestion at major centres—saving time and money.

Ideally located at Williamtown, between the urban centres of Newcastle and Port Stephens, the Airport is in the unique position of being jointly owned by these two Councils. Its outstanding success can be contributed to the Councils' decision to establish Newcastle Airport Limited to operate as a company reporting to an independent board. It is a highly successful arrangement which continues to reap dividends for both Councils and the region as a whole.

Like many operators in the thriving aviation industry, the Airport is a highly successful business and, under its charter, all profits are fed back into the continued improvement of infrastructure, and the marketing of the Airport and its facilities. In another unusual arrangement, Newcastle Airport shares runway facilities with the Williamtown RAAF base— home to Australia's FA-18 fighters. It is also home to manufacturing facilities for BAE Systems, with the Hawk Lead-In Fighters built within the boundaries of the Airport. As a result of these and other new partnerships, the private sector continues to benefit from considerable business opportunities.

In addition to the business and defence aspects of its operation, Newcastle Airport is conscious of its role in the tourism development of the region. Flexible and frequent transport links are a key factor in attracting new business and investment to the region but they are also an integral element in the development of tourism. Management at the Airport works closely with regional and state tourism organisations to maximise opportunities for growth throughout the Hunter.

Newcastle Airport is the aviation gateway linking the Hunter region with Australia and the rest of the world. While predominantly focused on domestic operations, it also has all the necessary facilities and customs requirements to cater for international flights.

As another commuter aircraft pulls up on the apron, another jet moves down the runway and takes flight. Newcastle Airport is a prime example of the new approach to business in the Hunter.

See page 178 for contact details >

NEWCASTLE
PORT CORPORATION

'The only certainty is change. As demands in world markets change, so do the needs of Hunter industries. It is the role of Newcastle Port Corporation to create business opportunities or respond to those industry needs, to ensure links between the region and world markets are efficient, effective and flexible.'

—Glen Oakley, CEO, Newcastle Port Corporation

First Port of Call

The two factors which have driven the development of Newcastle and the region since European settlement are its location on an extensive harbour at the mouth of the Hunter River, and the vast reserves of coal which extend from the coast to the Great Dividing Range.

The first commercial export from the fledgling colony of New South Wales, and the Australian continent was coal, shipped from the Port of Newcastle aboard the sailing ship *The Hunter*, bound for Bengal. Now, more than 200 years later, coal continues to dominate trade through the world's largest export coal port.

Without the nearby port, the coal industry in the Hunter may have been stifled by high transport costs. The subsequent development of the thriving city of Newcastle, the establishment of the steel industry, health, education and transport infrastructure, and the massive investment in aluminium production, would not have occurred but for the port.

Newcastle Port Corporation (NPC) is the primary economic driver for the region and a significant player in the world economy. International benchmarking studies have ranked the Port of Newcastle at the top of world productivity and quality performance scales for coal exports.

While the future of coal export remains bright, NPC has diversified the commodity base in recent years, and the pace of that diversification is increasing. Capital investments totalling $3 billion are currently under consideration and will ensure the future of the port as the crucial link between Hunter industries and their world markets.

Constant changes in the port, responding to evolving economic forces and hard-won efficiencies in shipping and materials handling has also enabled large tracts of harbourside land to be recycled, either for private redevelopment or the benefit of the community. The reclaimed expanse of the Foreshore and the exciting redevelopment of Honeysuckle are prime examples.

As manager of one of the primary drivers of the regional economy, NPC takes a leadership role in the community. It is a recognition that citizens, both corporate and individual, share a responsibility to work together to create a brighter future. NPC's contributions to environmental, arts and heritage projects, to charities as well as sporting and community events, clearly demonstrate that commitment.

On a prominent harbour headland, a striking statue welcomes ships from around the globe. Commissioned by NPC, the sculpture titled *Destiny* was inspired by the traditional figureheads on the bows of early sailing ships. This contemporary form embodies the spirit of the future of Newcastle, the region and NPC, stepping forward confidently, yet protecting the past.

See page 181 for contact details >

'The values of hard work and enterprise which underpinned Albert Toll's world in 1888 are ingrained in the company today. We have a strong interest in the Hunter, and not just because of its status as a key regional port in Australia. Part of having an eye on the future is remembering our past. The Hunter is a big part of both.'

—Steven Ford, General Manager, Toll Logistics, Ports and Resources Division

TOLL LOGISTICS

The Long Haul

The Toll story is a classic tale of 'local boy done good', from its humble Hunter beginnings to the major national leader in the ultra-competitive transport logistics industry.

Founded by Albert Toll in Newcastle in 1888, the company began hauling coal with horse and cart. It became part of the Peko Wallsend Group in the 1960s, transporting equipment for diversified mining and manufacturing activities.

From 1986, the Toll's course changed dramatically when it was sold to a management buyout team led by current managing director Paul Little. The brand has progressively grown through acquisitions and organic growth to become Australia's leading 'integrated total logistics provider'.

Toll maintains a keen interest in Newcastle and the Hunter today. The region remains the home of Toll Logistics' Ports and Resources Division, managing supply chains for high profile clients locally, and in far reaching places across Australia, from Kalgoorlie to the north-west shelf, all from their offices in Newcastle.

In its own backyard, Toll is a joint partner in the Eastern Basin Distribution Centre, the first major step in the revitalisation of port operations in the Hunter. Toll's proven long-term investment strategy in the region ensures it will continue to be a part of the changing face of the city's port-related activities as regional facilities more and more become a viable alternative to capital cities.

See page 186 for contact details >

UNITED GONINAN

'Supporting Newcastle for more than 100 years, United Goninan are leaders in rail vehicle design manufacturing, modernisation and maintenance. As part of United Group Limited, Goninan continues its proud history now as United Goninan. With 14 operations throughout Australia and South-East Asia and over 1,200 employees, United Goninan is committed to the growth and development of its business, employees and the Hunter region.'

—Allan Smith, Managing Director, United Goninan

See page 187 for contact details >

121

seven

A LEARNING CITY

Newcastle is fast becoming a centre for educational excellence, offering innovative educational options for students and scoring international research successes.

partners

'Excellent partnerships operate in Newcastle ... resulting in outstanding opportunities for a world-class education and professional training experience, cutting-edge research and research training, excellent health services and close and effective collaboration with local business and university.'

—Professor Roger Holmes, Vice Chancellor, University of Newcastle

The revolutionary changes under way in the Hunter Valley have not been confined to the factory gates. Equally important if more subtle changes have been wrought behind the scenes in the region's educational institutions, which have become willing and cooperative partners in the blooming of Newcastle as a 'learning city'.

Three key players—the University of Newcastle, the Hunter Institute of Technology and the Hunter Area Health Service—are cooperating for the benefit of the region. Together with organisations such as the Hunter Urban Division of General Practice, they are creating innovative educational options for students and are opening doors to the world of international research success.

The links between schools, higher education, private industry and the wider community mean that traditional paths for students—high school, followed by TAFE for a trade qualification or university for an academic degree—are changing. The new flexibility in the education system allows students to 'stream' between institutions.

Higher School Certificate modules are on offer at the Hunter Institute of Technology, while high school music students can study at the Newcastle Conservatorium of Music under the administration of University of Newcastle. The Hunter Institute, the University of Newcastle and the District Office of School Education run Callaghan College, a specialised secondary facility created by the amalgamation of three Newcastle high schools.

The Hunter Institute accepts and values workplace experience in assessing 'recognition of prior learning' concessions to its students. Students who apply to the University of Newcastle are given generous credits for the qualifications gained at any of the institute's 16 campuses.

Many of Hunter Health's medical staff hold academic positions at the university and the institute, and a combined research effort coordinated by the Hunter Medical Research Institute (HMRI) is breaking new ground in a number of important areas.

University Vice Chancellor Professor Roger Holmes says the changes in Newcastle since he arrived in the mid-1990s have been dramatic. 'Newcastle has had an image as a working class town and although it's not something I think we should move away from all together, we need people to realise that this is an area where education and innovation go hand in hand, where the cooperation between the various players gives us a united front.'

On a weekday morning, traffic into the university is some of the heaviest that Newcastle ever sees. Students arrive in droves by bus and car on one side of the campus, while on the other, trains pull into the university station.

The University of Newcastle is one of Australia's largest regional universities

University of Newcastle attracts many overseas students who often choose to stay and work in the area.

with 20,000 students, placing it fifteenth in terms of size. The university has a cosmopolitan feel, largely due to its ability to attract overseas students. Nearly 10 per cent of the student population comes from abroad and many of these fee-paying students retain links with the city once their formal education is over.

The University of Newcastle boasts an enviable education and research record, ranking ninth out of 38 institutions, something for which Vice Chancellor Roger Holmes is extremely proud.

'We are working towards a substantial increase in the numbers of students doing PhDs and Masters coursework,'

Roger Holmes says. Together with his senior colleagues at the Hunter Institute of Technology and Hunter Health, he believes strongly in the importance of strong academic links with the community.

'As Vice Chancellor I like to see the university involved in as many major commercial and industrial projects as possible. We work closely with the local councils, the state and federal governments, and the university is represented on any number of corporate and community boards and advisory groups,' Roger Holmes says.

One of the University of Newcastle's most high-profile successes is its

medical school, which has helped usher in a new era of medical teaching around the country. The faculty departs from convention in two main ways. First, the assessment process uses much more than Year 12 exam results when selecting its first year intake. Potential students are interviewed by a panel of medical and non-medical personnel and places are reserved for mature-age and Aboriginal students. Second, traditional rote-teaching methods have been displaced by 'problem-based' learning; students are encouraged to work through problems in real-life situations. These methods were initially viewed with caution by many in the medical profession, but the 'Newcastle approach' is gaining favour around the world. This approach is also being adopted in other faculties, including architecture, building and social work.

'Problem-based learning, or evidence-based practice, takes learning out of the purely theoretical, fact-repeating frameworks of the past and allows students to absorb information through applying their knowledge in a practical sense,' Roger Holmes says.

research

The Hunter Medical Research Institute (HMRI) was established in 1998 as a multi-campus institute bringing together researchers from the University of Newcastle and the Hunter Area Health Service.

The institute's executive director Professor John Rostas says that with 300 researchers and staff working across the lower Hunter, HMRI is the only organisation of its type in New South Wales (NSW) outside of Sydney.

Grants to HMRI researchers total about $12 million a year, while the state government provides more than $950,000 a year in infrastructure funding, an amount set to double in coming years as the institute matures.

HMRI has six areas of research: cancer, pregnancy and childbirth, clinical neurosciences, mucosal immunology and respiratory diseases, cardio-vascular medicine, and public health.

stuart pianos

In the same way that the name Steinway has dominated the world of pianos for the past century, the name Stuart is set to have the same effect in the 21st century.

The Stuart piano is a true revolution in design, built in Newcastle by inventor, piano technician Wayne Stuart, and backed by the Newcastle Conservatorium of Music, the CSIRO and the University of Newcastle's commercial research arm, TUNRA Ltd.

The technological breakthrough that gives the Stuart its revolutionary sound came to its designer in 1989. Conventional piano strings are bent around bridge pins, but this bend means the vibration moves eventually into the horizontal as well as vertical plane, accelerating the speed at which the sound dies away. In the Stuart, the strings are supported in agraffes, which eliminate the side-to-side string movement inherent in conventional designs. This means the strings vibrate for longer, producing a distinctively clear, bright and dynamic sound.

The Stuart piano has come to prominence as a result of a three-year project by pianist Gerard Willems and producer Brendan Ward, who set out to record the entire catalogue of Beethoven's piano works. After an initially sceptical reception, the Stuart began to receive the accolades it deserves. The first half of the 10-CD opus won an ARIA (Australian Recording Industry Association) award for classical music and led to a steady stream of international musicians visiting Newcastle to sample the instrument's subtle beauty.

'The Stuart piano is a demonstration to the world of Newcastle's capacity in so many areas. Of course there is the obvious technological side, which embraces advanced engineering and manufacturing, but the artistic side is in some ways even more astonishing. What we have shown the world is that rare combination of a world-class instrument, an acoustically brilliant concert hall at the conservatorium and the brilliant skills and artistry of our pianists. And all of it is here, in Newcastle,' says Professor Robert Constable, head of the Newcastle Conservatorium of Music.

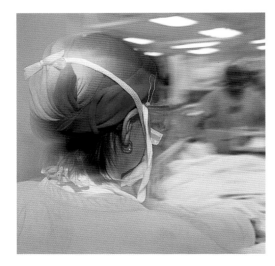

The Hunter Valley has a proud history of community funding for medical research, typified by the millions of dollars raised over the years by the high-profile NBN Television telethons.

HMRI and its youth fundraising wing, Pulse, have attracted more than $2 million from individual and corporate donors in just two years. A result that John Rostas sees as clear evidence of the institute's community support.

He believes there are good reasons for researchers to choose the Hunter as a base. Apart from lifestyle advantages, he believes there is a much better nexus between health services and researchers in Newcastle.

'The reason for this is that we have one health service and one university covering the entire area ... The demarcation disputes—access to patients, fights over intellectual property—don't happen here. And to top it off, we enjoy a degree of community support that the rest of Australia just can't match.'

trade

Newcastle and the Hunter region's industrial strength is reflected in the higher than average percentage of trade qualifications. The Hunter Institute of Technology administers a range of full-time and part-time courses from vocational education through to trade level, associate diploma and certificate level. Its cooperation with the region's other key educators and innovative approach to skills training have seen a number of recent successes.

The region's education providers have worked hard in the past decade to make the system more flexible, practical and focused on results. 'The educational resources of this region [are now seen as] one entity, rather than distinct or discrete paths, as was previously the case,' Gaye Hart, Hunter Institute Director, says.

The institute plays an important role in providing trained personnel to Newcastle and Hunter Valley businesses, especially in the all-important field of information technology (IT). It offers 35 IT qualifications and student numbers are steadily growing. As an educator of 5,000 students a year, the institute is crucial to the community as both a provider of skills resources and as a major economic entity.

Gaye Hart says that companies wishing to establish in the Hunter Valley can count on the institute as a partner in building a workforce. The institute works with employers and students to develop skills training to meet employers' immediate needs, providing work-ready staff. It can even help access government funding in assist in training.

'We will not simply give you a hit of information technology training and get out again. We will actually help you identify what you need over the long term as well as the short term. We will be there as part of a long-term partnership,' she says.

The institute's boat and shipbuilding course is one example of the way the institute works with industry for the benefit of the community. Initially the course faced pressure to shut down due to lack of student numbers and the relevance of the coursework.

'The problem wasn't in a lack of boats being built, it was with us. We weren't teaching the skills that modern boat builders need,' Gaye Hart says. Following consultation with boatbuilders in the region, the course was refocused to meet potential employers' needs.

'Now we have more than 80 apprentices enrolled and parts of the course are delivered on-site at the individual boatbuilding businesses.'

'Hunter Health is improving the health of people in the Hunter with its vast network of services, from community health to in-patient hospital services, from disease prevention activities to high-level trauma care. Health services here really are world-class.'

—Professor Katherine McGrath, Chief Executive Officer, Hunter Health

NEWCASTLE HEALTH SERVICES

The good health of Hunter people is guaranteed, thanks to unique collaborative relationships between Hunter Health (Hunter Area Health Service), the Hunter Urban Division of General Practice (HUDGP), the University of Newcastle, the Hunter Medical Research Institute (HMRI) and the community.

Hunter Health's Chief Executive Officer, Professor Katherine McGrath, said the partnerships stemmed from the stimulating and dynamic environment provided by the city of Newcastle.

'It's big enough to have the resources, the infrastructure and the critical mass for world class health services, medical research and education, but small enough so organisations that may otherwise work in isolation can come together. The result is excellent health services for all.'

The partnership between Hunter Health and the HUDGP is leading to the development of world class innovation in health care

systems and information management, in addition to better health services.

'The cooperative links between these two organisations have led to outstanding health care. A commitment to the needs of our region and a proudly parochial "can do" spirit have led the way in overturning traditional barriers to collaborative health care,' said HUDGP Executive Director, Dr Arn Sprogis.

The vision for a united and innovative health system, pioneered by Professor McGrath and Dr Sprogis, is becoming recognised as a model of best practice across the state and even Australia.

Hunter Health and the University of Newcastle, particularly the Faculty of Medicine and Health Sciences, are linked in a number of ways, including conjoint appointments between the two organisations and the development of the Hunter Medical Research Institute (HMRI).

Opposite, from top: Services for expectant mums in Newcastle are world class. John Hunter Hospital and The John Hunter Children's Hospital are co-located which means specialist care is available to both mum and baby on the one site, should it be needed; staff at work in one of nine operating theatres at Newcastle's John Hunter Hospital, a tertiary referral teaching hospital affiliated with The University of Newcastle; Professor John Rostas, Executive Director of the Hunter Medical Research Institute.

The University's international reputation as a centre of excellence in medical education has also resulted in global recognition of health services and medical research in the Hunter, according to the University's Vice Chancellor and President, Professor Roger Holmes.

'The Hunter Medical Research Institute illustrates what can be achieved when like-minded groups collaborate,' said HMRI Executive Director Professor John Rostas.

'HMRI came together as a partnership between the University of Newcastle, Hunter Health and the business community. These groups share a vision of a Hunter future that has medical research contributing not only better health and globally significant medical research results, but also economic wealth to the city.'

The HMRI has 300 researchers across seven campuses, including the University of Newcastle and various Hunter Health facilities. Businesses have provided financial and practical support via the Top 200 campaign, with many leading Hunter firms nominating HMRI as their preferred charity. Newcastle's support of charitable causes is legendary and the community's support of HMRI is no exception.

There is no doubt that the level of cooperation across Newcastle's health sector is building prosperity through partnership for the people of this city and beyond.

See page 179 for contact details >

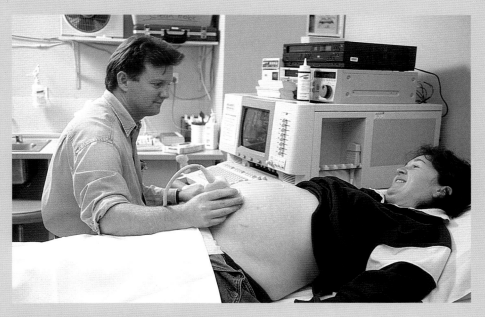

'AOK Health is an innovative exporter of products and services designed and tested in the Hunter. We provide continuing education programs for professional and corporate clients across Australia. Our teaching and service staff hold qualifications in a range of rehabilitation and sports sciences.'

—Bradley Wilson, Managing Director, AOK Health Pty Ltd

AOK HEALTH PTY LTD

Take a simple idea. Refine it. Insist on quality. Educate customers of the benefits. Add a liberal measure of determination. That's been the formula for success of one of the Hunter region's innovative companies, AOK Health.

Established in 1995, AOK Health designs, develops, markets and distributes innovative health and fitness products, and education services, both in Australia and overseas, from its headquarters in Newcastle. The company has export contracts to the United States, England, Canada, New Zealand, Indonesia, Malaysia, Singapore, Hong Kong and Fiji.

One of AOK's major product successes in the international marketplace is a training and rehabilitation tool known as mediBall PRO, developed as a result of materials testing and evaluation of ball products by the University of Newcastle's Materials Testing

Laboratory. The brightly coloured balls, up to 85cm in diameter, are used as ergonomic seating or as a tool in occupational health and safety exercises and rehabilitation programs.

AOK Health incorporates a philosophy of 'self-care' into its products and services, believing that education and self-management are critical in reducing the burden on health services around the world and improving corporate productivity.

For AOK, the Hunter region has proven to be a great launching pad for business. The proximity of a world-class research establishment at the University of Newcastle and a proactive and dynamic local business community has meant lower comparable overheads and capital costs to help fund business growth.

See page 172 for contact details >

'The Delta EMD plant at Newcastle is a world-class operation in terms of performance, quality and the environment. All activities are directed towards one single aim—meeting the needs of our customers—hence our strong commitment to research partnerships with major battery manufacturers.'

—Evan van Zyl, Chairman and Managing Director, Delta EMD Australia Pty Limited

DELTA EMD AUSTRALIA PTY LIMITED

Energy on the Move

The steadily growing world demand for portable electrical energy to power an increasing array of devices means a bright future for the Newcastle plant of Delta EMD.

Delta is the world's largest producer of electrolytic manganese dioxide (EMD), used to make dry-cell batteries. From its plants in South Africa and Australia, Delta supplies a product which meets the toughest demands of the battery industry's leading manufacturers.

It is an advanced chemical engineering process which demands the highest standards of state-of-the-art systems and the people who operate them. For Delta EMD, Newcastle is an ideal location, with excellent port and rail infrastructure and strong engineering skill resources. The plant also has firm ties to The University of Newcastle, matching Delta EMD's commitment to research partnerships with leading battery producers. These partnerships mean Delta is well placed to be a leading supplier of high-quality EMD for the next generation of dry cell batteries, including lithium ion and alkaline batteries for high drain applications.

The dedication to quality throughout the Newcastle operation is matched only by the commitment to protection of the local environment. Continuing research is revealing new ways to process by-products for recycling and re-use.

See page 173 for contact details >

133

'The future of education and training lies in our ability to share our strengths and broaden the opportunities for all.'

—Dr Gaye Hart, Director, Hunter Institute of Technology and Professor Roger Holmes, Vice Chancellor & President, The University of Newcastle

HUNTER INSTITUTE OF TECHNOLOGY—TAFE NSW
THE UNIVERSITY OF NEWCASTLE

In the Hunter, two outstanding educational institutions—The University of Newcastle and the Hunter Institute of Technology (TAFE NSW)—are major providers of post secondary education for the region. They work together and with other sectors of education to offer the best opportunities to students through especially developed pathways that recognise prior learning and provide accreditation for completed awards.

The University of Newcastle is ranked fourth among the 12 universities in New South Wales in its ability to attract first preferences for those enrolling in undergraduate programs. Its success in winning major government research funding is also significant, ranking ninth out of the 36 public universities in Australia. Major study areas include architecture, building, design, arts, social science, economics, business and commerce, education, engineering, law, medicine and health sciences, music, nursing, science and mathematics.

Hunter Institute of Technology is one of the largest and most enterprising TAFE Institutes in Australia. Through its ongoing collaboration with the community and the industry sector, the Institute has adopted a leading role in supporting regional development within a global economic environment.

The Institute has a proud reputation of excellence in teaching and learning and has positioned itself as a leader in the national vocational education and training system.

The Institute offers more than 500 courses in a number of career disciplines.

See page 176 for contact details >

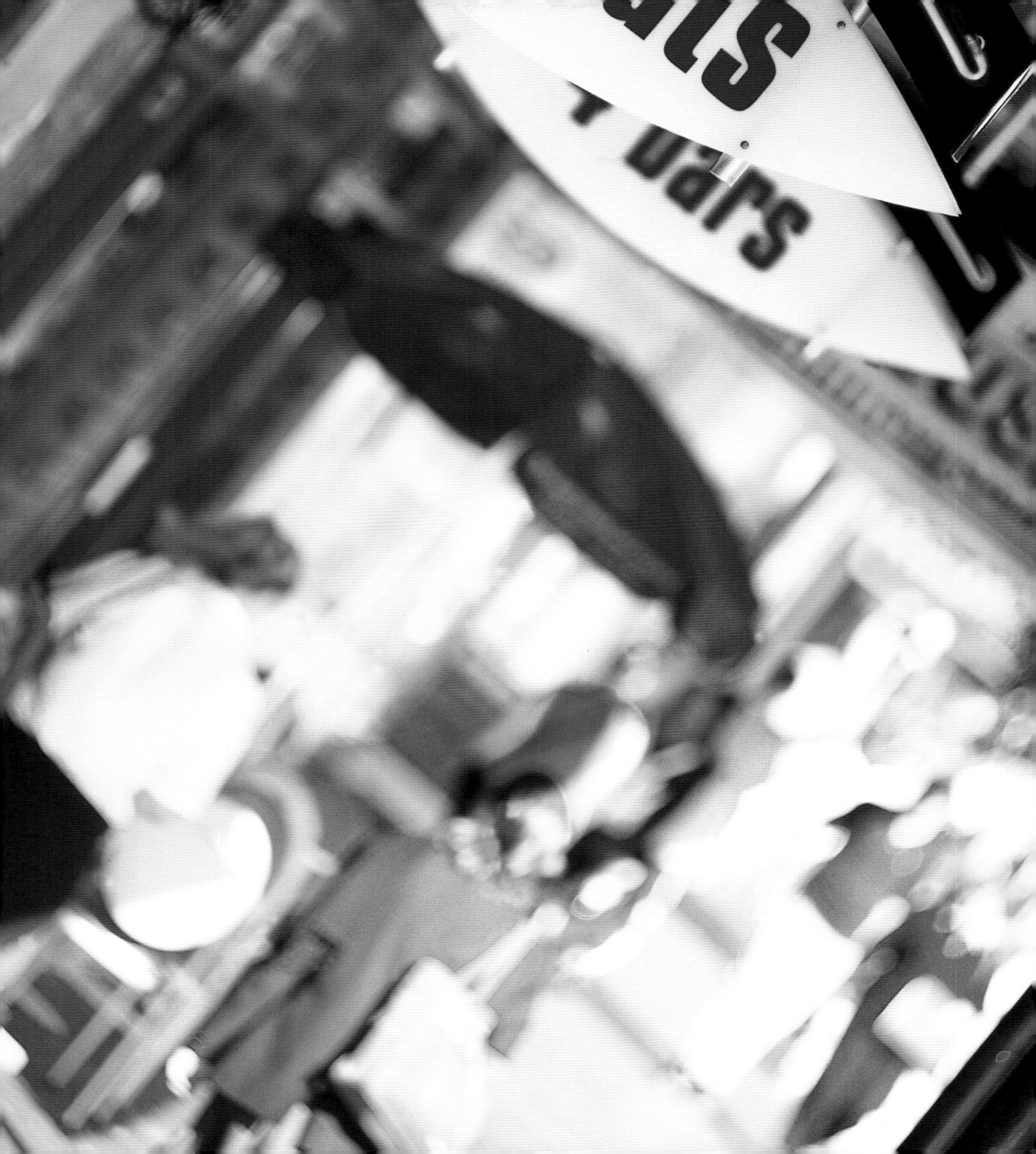
bars

eight
FUTURE DEVELOPMENT

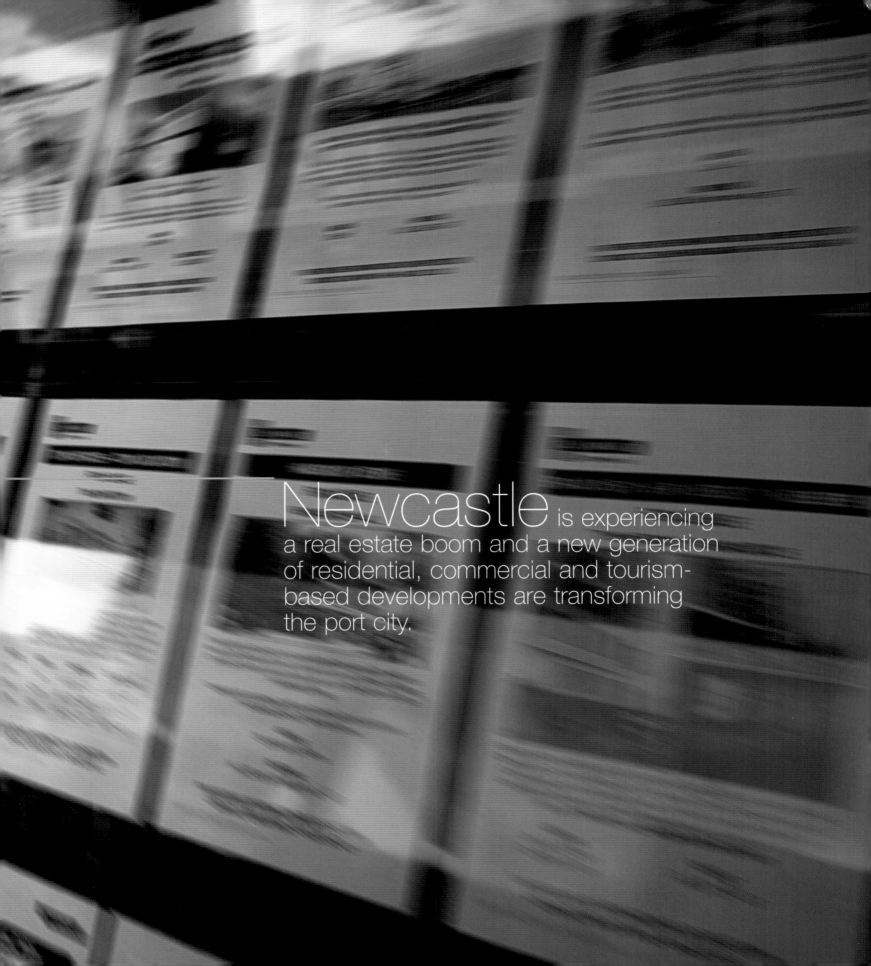

Newcastle is experiencing a real estate boom and a new generation of residential, commercial and tourism-based developments are transforming the port city.

The 1989 earthquake was the trigger for Newcastle's real estate boom. All told, an estimated 60,000 houses and buildings in the region suffered some form of structural damage, including half of the structures in Newcastle's central business district (CBD). A real estate renaissance began and there has been a steady rise in median house prices ever since.

Newcastle's property market started to reflect changing shopping habits, as the city's new suburban shopping centres replaced the CBD as the centre of retail activity in the mid-1990s. The decline in retail real estate in the CBD precipitated a revival of residential development that is changing the face of the city.

'The biggest change in Newcastle is that we are more mature, we are prepared to take on challenges in a more positive way in terms of dealing with rapid change.'

—Councillor John S Tate, Lord Mayor, The City of Newcastle

Former landmark office buildings were converted into townhouses and a string of impressive new apartment blocks sprung up across the CBD. Early developments were encouraged by a shop-top housing policy developed by Newcastle City Council; this policy was eventually merged into the Development Control Plan governing construction in the city. The trickle of first-floor renovations soon became a flood. In 2000 alone, the council approved residential developments in central Newcastle worth more than $150 million.

For more than a century, the narrow strip of harbour-front land between Hunter Street and the harbour was a maze of goods-based railway lines and heavy wooden wharves dotted with cranes. Changing trade and transport needs had long rendered such infrastructure redundant, and in the early 1980s the first stage of redevelopment of this crucial area was undertaken as part of Australia's bicentenary celebrations.

Foreshore Park has become a Newcastle landmark. Tens of thousands regularly gather on the foreshore for holiday celebration concerts and fireworks displays. On summer weekends especially, the Foreshore is alive with picnicking families taking advantage of the manicured and shaded lawns and playgrounds. A paved promenade (below) runs along the water's edge from the famed Nobbys breakwall. The main navigation channels of the busy harbour are only a stone's throw from the waters' edge, giving passers-by close views of some of the world's biggest cargo ships in motion.

Newcastle harbour has always been a beautiful port, but its industrial importance meant it was all but overlooked as a recreational playground. The Foreshore Park whetted the Novocastrian appetite for a beautiful waterfront and Honeysuckle, the city's biggest redevelopment project, is dedicated to satisfying that craving.

Honeysuckle's brief is to transform more than 50 hectares of surplus New South Wales (NSW) government land running along four kilometres of harbour foreshore in a boomerang shaped strip from the inner-city suburbs

Scratchleys Restaurant is one of a number of businesses bringing new life to the harbour.

of Civic to Wickham. This area was nothing more than a run down maze of railway goods sidings, derelict wharves and redundant woolsheds.

A series of splendid Victorian railway buildings and warehouses have been retained on Honeysuckle's eastern tip, but the rest of the site has been cleared in preparation for a new generation of residential, commercial and tourism-based developments. Allocation has also been made for public space; 32 per cent or 16 hectares of the site will be dedicated as open space with a foreshore promenade allowing unbroken public access from Throsby Creek to Nobbys breakwall.

Honeysuckle will house at least 3,000 people. A series of medium density residential projects have already been built at Wickham and Carrington, which have spurred privately funded urban renewal in nearby streets.

Newcastle has become a prominent convention destination in recent years and one of the most eagerly awaited aspects of Honeysuckle is the $75 million four-star hotel, convention centre and apartment complex being built by Melbourne-based Becton Corporation. The Crowne Plaza Hotel on Merewether Wharf will rise over the harbour waterfront at Honeysuckle's eastern end, offering views out to the sea

and over the coast north of Newcastle to Port Stephens.

Other exciting Honeysuckle projects include a $20 million waterfront restaurant and retail centre, immediately west of the hotel, to be built by Newcastle developer Stronach. Farther upstream, developer Buildev is due to start work on another $20 million project, the landmark Honeysuckle House. Nearby in Hunter Street, developer Accor has won approval for an $8 million Ibis motel adjacent to an apartment block being undertaken by Newcastle developer JML.

eco-park

BHP executives knew that the Newcastle steelworks plant was unlikely to continue operation into the new millennium. With this in mind, the company's Newcastle management cast around for an appropriate gesture with which to commemorate its eight-decade relationship with the city.

In 1996 BHP executives and the NSW government announced the Steel River project, an 'eco-industrial' park to be built on 104 hectares of BHP land upstream from the main steelworks site between the south arm of the Hunter River and Industrial Highway, the road skirting the steelworks. Central to the eco-industrial philosophy is the idea that emissions from various Steel River industries are treated as components of a park-wide 'environmental envelope'. This envelope, with detailed emission limits for a vast range of potential emissions, was worked out in the planning stages between BHP, the community and New South Wales government departments including the NSW Environment Protection Authority. The 'environmental envelope' emission system is married to special planning regulations that promise approval for complying businesses within 28 days of lodging a Development Application, breaking new ground in property development.

*Right: Kooragang Island is home to a wetland
reserve and BHP's former landholding on the
island is being remediated.*

In early 2001, Steel River was purchased by a group of Newcastle investors, under the name Steel River Pty Ltd. Spokesman and Director Ross Wilson says the new owners are dedicated to carrying on the 'Steel River vision', developed over more than two years of consultation with neighbouring residents, environmentalists and other special interest groups.

Steel River's directors see a mixture of small-lot subdivisions interspersed with major tenants as the 104-hectare park's vision becomes reality. 'We see a mixture of industries, laboratories and offices, tending more to the high-tech end than heavy industry itself,' Ross Wilson says.

Nearly $20 million has gone into site development and infrastructure provision at Steel River, and a 20 hectare first stage is on the market with lots from 2,500 square metres upwards.

The CSIRO, Australia's premier science organisation, is the park's first major tenant, with a $25 million energy research centre planned for a prominent five-hectare site on a hill in the park's south-eastern corner.

Steel River is not the only industrial site in Newcastle and the surrounding region. At Kurri Kurri, the proposed Hunter Employment Zone, commonly known as Tomalpin, is in the early planning stages and has the support of the Cessnock City Council.

Changing planning philosophies mean that large buffer zones established around Upper Hunter power stations and the Tomago Aluminum smelter are also being opened up to heavy industry. The Tomago zone is partially owned by the company and partially owned by the NSW government.

Macquarie Generation owns about 9,000 hectares around the Bayswater and Liddell power stations, and several sites in this area have been set aside for industrial use.

Maitland property developer Hilton Grugeon is one of the region's quiet achievers. His first major Hunter project, the Cardiff industrial estate, is now home to dozens of businesses that employ hundreds of people. Grugeon's current project, Hunter Land's Thornton industrial estate, is repeating the Cardiff success on a larger scale. The centrepiece of the estate is the Hunter Transport Centre, a 'transport hub' assisted in its early stages by a $1.5 million grant from the Australian government's Newcastle Structural Adjustment Fund.

'The transport centre is the coming together in the one site of all of the facilities needed to run heavy transport, from semi-trailers to buses,' Hilton Grugeon says.

'There are various automotive businesses, such as auto-electricians, spare parts suppliers, truck and bus maintenance companies, food suppliers, even a small motel accommodation service for drivers to shower and sleep.

'Mercedes has its truck and bus sales and service department here, and there are at the moment five major transport companies based here, including Finlays, Tri State and Towers Transport.'

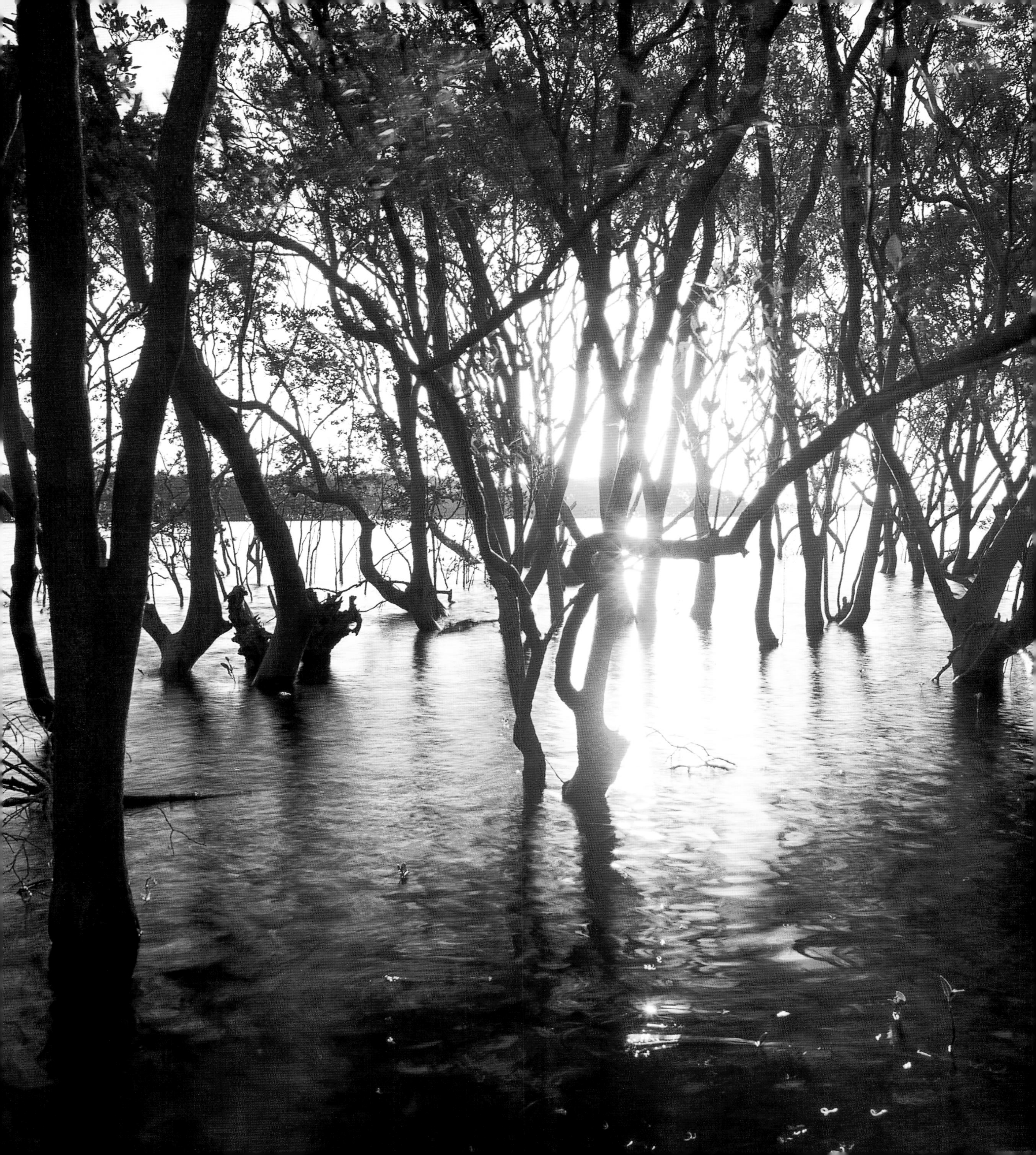

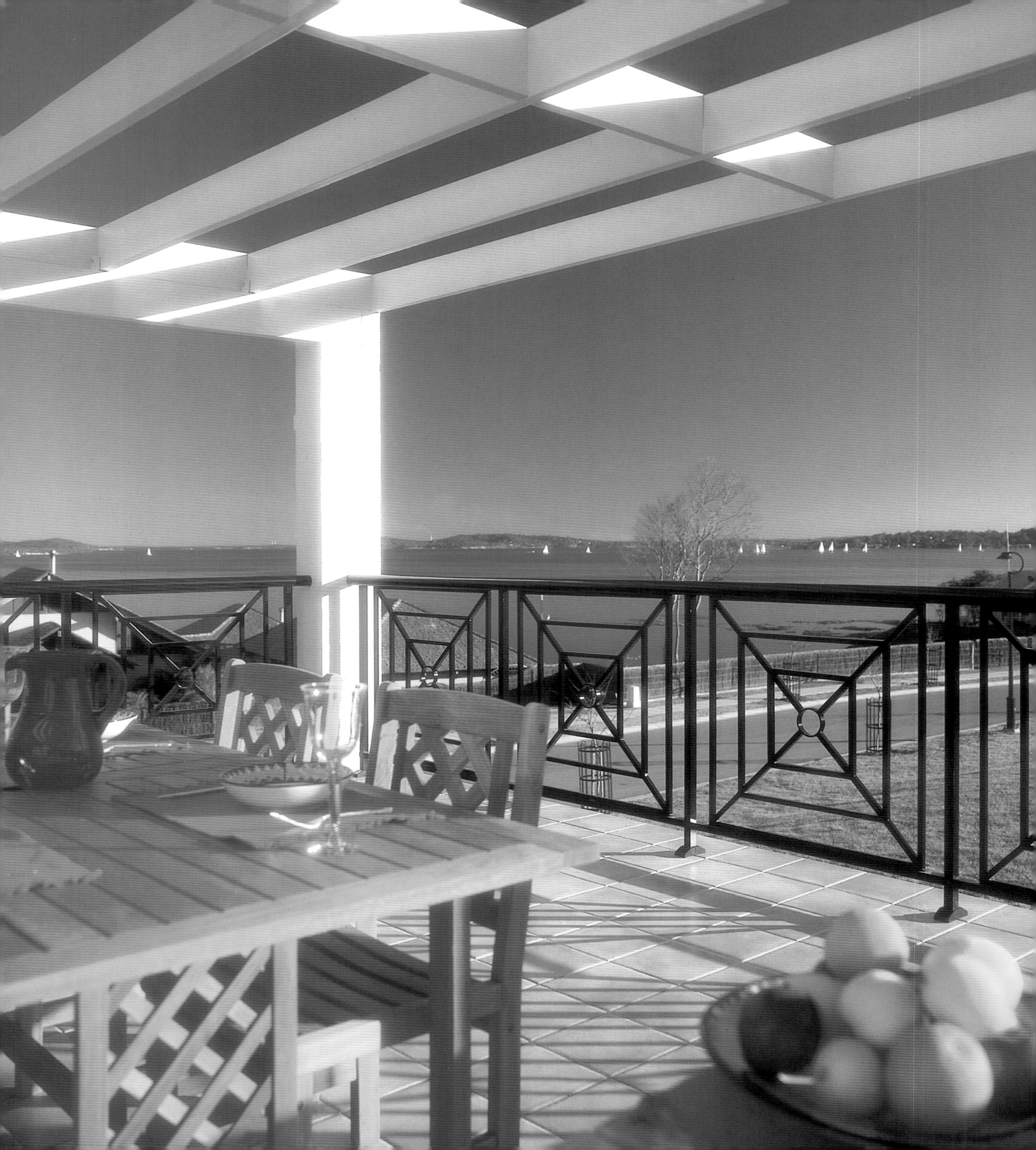

reuse

In its eight decades in Newcastle, BHP gradually became the largest single landholder in the region. Even after disposing of many of its assets, including a string of coalmines that once provided coking coal for the Newcastle steelworks, it still held more than 2,300 hectares in and around Newcastle.

Midway through 2000, BHP and the NSW government began negotiations to transfer BHP's four main holdings into public ownership together with a package of funding to cover the cost of remediation where needed. The four parcels are:

- 150 hectares of steelworks land at Port Waratah;
- 230 hectares of former steelworks waste management land on Kooragang Island;
- 500 hectares of former sandmining foreshore at Belmont; and
- 500 hectares of former coalmining land at West Wallsend.

Demolition has begun on the steelworks site, which will become the Port of Newcastle's new multi-purpose shipping terminal (MPT).

Part of the Belmont land is likely to be preserved as a foreshore and wetland park, while the Kooragang land is likely to be remediated and opened up to industry, as it is adjacent to some of the Port's most important industries. West Wallsend land at the western side of the F3 Freeway north from Sydney is likely to be used for housing.

A wild bush-covered headland and underground coalmine with a controversial history, Green Point was bought by one of the region's biggest building companies, the McCloy Group, in 1992.

Lake Macquarie City Council owned 40 hectares of Green Point, and there was a substantial push from residents and the green lobby for the entire headland to be bought by the council

or government. In a deal that McCloy spokesman Ross Howard says offered a 'clear win-win' situation, the company handed 120 hectares of its 180 hectare holding to the council, and was granted permission to develop the remaining 60 hectares.

Today, McCloy's Green Point development is nearly two-thirds complete; it will eventually run to 550 sites to be developed in 15 stages.

The foreshore park includes more than 2 kilometres of absolute waterfront, with some of the best views on the Lake. Green Point has quickly become a prestige address and property prices across the estate have risen steadily since the project began.

'We've all learnt a lot out of a project of this type and it has set the standard around here for sustainable residential development in a potentially sensitive environment,' Ross Howard says.

Opposite: Former industrial sites around Lake Macquarie are being remediated to make way for luxury developments such as Green Point.

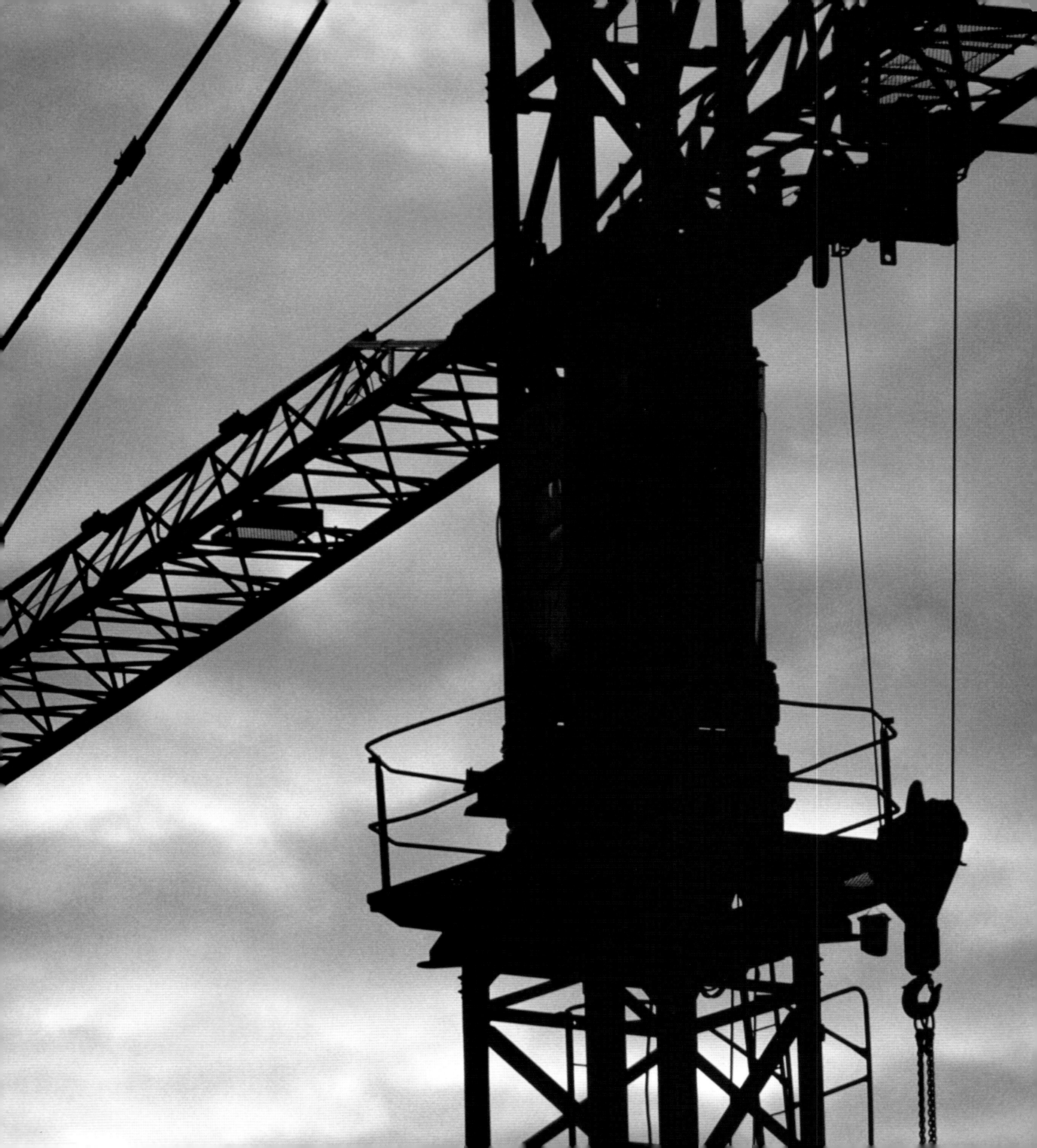

'Experience on a wide variety of major projects in the Hunter region has given Daracon the skills and capability to keep on winning major contracts. The company's commitment to quality, safety and the environment ensures the company is a leader in the industry.'

—David Mingay, Managing Director, Daracon Group

DARACON ENGINEERING PTY LTD

Precision Development

There are few companies which can rightfully claim to have played a role in most major development and infrastructure projects in the Hunter region in the past two decades. The Daracon Group can certainly justify such a claim, with a proud track record on projects as diverse as extension of the F3 Freeway, the Charlestown Square and Garden City shopping complexes and expansion of the coal loader on Kooragang Island.

The Wallsend-based engineering group also played a key role in the $80 million major works for the Sydney 2000 Olympic Games at Stadium Australia, the Aquatic Centre, new showground facilities, the Equestrian Centre, Olympic Village, media village and much more.

The company now boasts over 250 employees from engineers and surveyors to plant operators and landscape gardeners and horticulturalists. Working on complex projects such as a golf course and resort development, major subdivisions and road construction, it is a far cry from the origins of Daracon in 1983, with two working directors, an operator and one grader.

Group Managing Director David Mingay knows that the Hunter region is a great base to build a strong, competitive business. 'This is a tough market, but there are plenty of opportunities. We've made the most of those opportunities and built a company which can compete and win against the best in Australia.'

See page 173 for contact details >

NEWCASTLE:BUSINESS

HONEYSUCKLE DEVELOPMENT CORPORATION

'There are terrific development opportunities at Honeysuckle, a major catalyst for the re-imaging and revitalisation of inner Newcastle. Over 20 years the Honeysuckle redevelopment project will inject dollars into the regional economy, create new jobs and attract more new residents to the inner city.'

—David Le Marchant, Chairman, Honeysuckle Development Corporation

See page 175 for contact details >

W STRONACH PTY LTD

'Since 1927, when William Stronach laid the foundations for the grand Civic Theatre, the Stronach name has been synonymous with building excellence, with a reputation for professionalism, trust and loyalty, reinvesting in the future of the region with an innovative approach to the entire development process, from design to financing of major projects.'

—Keith Stronach, Managing Director, W Stronach Pty Ltd

Above from top: The Civic Theatre, Newcastle, 1927; Tower Winery and Lodge, Hunter Valley.

See page 188 for contact details >

NEWCASTLE:BUSINESS

nine
A GREAT PLACE TO LIVE

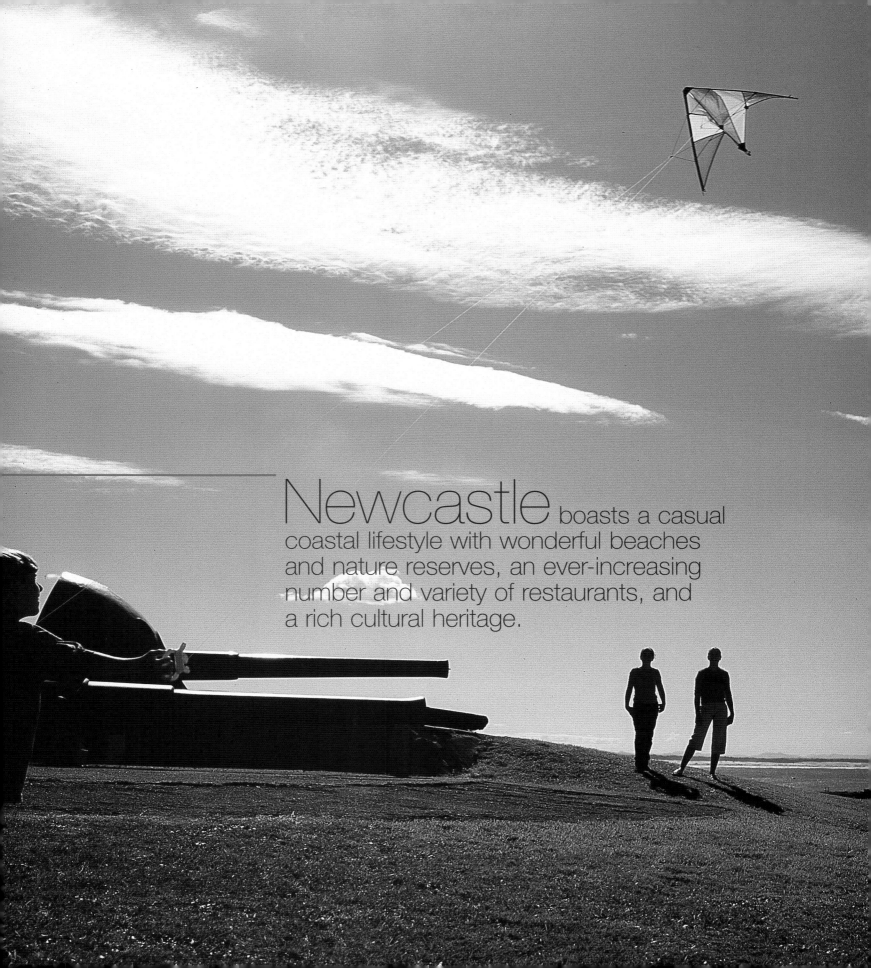

Newcastle boasts a casual
coastal lifestyle with wonderful beaches
and nature reserves, an ever-increasing
number and variety of restaurants, and
a rich cultural heritage.

Newcastle has wonderful hospitals, an internationally renowned university and the largest art gallery outside of a capital city. It has beautiful beaches and nature reserves, and boasts three times the national average of open space per person. It also has above-average home ownership rates and Australia's lowest cost of living based on food and grocery indexes.

It is home to one of Australia's largest collections of intact Victorian and Federation streetscapes, which received a facelift following the December 1989 earthquake that rocked the city. The $2 billion rebuilding program that followed breathed new life into the inner city.

'People frequently mention the lifestyle as a positive attribute to the city. It is home to some of the most beautiful beaches in Australia, a vibrant arts and cultural community, a top class university, extensive health and medical facilities ... parks and gardens, easy transport accessibility and a maritime environment influenced by an active working port.'

—Janet Dore, General Manager, The City of Newcastle

Newcastle's café and restaurant precincts are thriving.

The city's various restaurant strips are alive with diners and revellers seven days, and nights, a week. As inner Newcastle enters a new phase as a burgeoning residential area, restaurants and cafes are doing a roaring trade.

The established 'eat streets' are Beaumont Street, Hamilton, and Darby Street, Cooks Hill. Hamilton has long been a multicultural suburb and has always had its share of cafes, particularly along Beaumont Street, but it was a sleepy area that closed early and stayed quiet on weekends. Beaumont Street has since transformed and it is one of the most talked-about changes in modern Newcastle. The ravaged street picked itself up in early-1990, following the devastation of the earthquake, and has sprung to life.

The long-standing Italian and Greek restaurants frequented by generations of migrant steelworkers now sit comfortably next to Thai, Vietnamese, French, Turkish, African and South American restaurants. More than 100 restaurants are packed into half a dozen blocks. The footpaths are crowded every night of the week and the hotels rollick with music. Weekend jazz and food festivals attract tens of thousands of people at a time.

Beaumont Street is also facing some stiff competition. The Junction, at the corner of Union Street and Glebe Road, boasts a cosmopolitan selection, as does The Foreshore around Queens Wharf. The latest 'restaurant row' is in Newcastle East. Clustered around the Essington Apartments, a landmark conversion of a former Royal Newcastle Hospital nurses' quarters, it features an eclectic array of new eateries.

Bar Beach attracts crowds of people in summer.

beaches

Newcastle possesses all of the varied beauty that the NSW coast is renowned for the world over. The main city in the Hunter region, it is the state's second most popular tourism destination after Sydney. The region is lucky enough to possess one of the world's great stretches of coastline and the temperate climate is ideal for recreation.

From the wild, isolated beauty of Seal Rocks to the north and the similarly undeveloped Catherine Hill Bay and Fraser Park to the south, the coast is a picture postcard strip of beautiful sandy beaches and spectacular rocks and cliffs.

Crowds of swimmers take to the waves at city beaches in warmer months, but it is not hard to find a quiet swimming spot even on the hottest of days. The surf life saving movement is extremely strong in the Hunter, and most of the region's beaches are patrolled during summer. Newcastle has long had a reputation as a 'Surf City', and the annual Surfest boardriding contest has grown into one of professional surfing's most popular events.

Mark Richards won professional surfing's world championship four times in the 1970s. He still surfs with awe-inspiring skill and he remains a city favourite, a genuine sporting icon.

Mark Richards' Hunter Street board shop is a meeting place for many of the sport's leading up-and-comers. While a younger generation of Newcastle pros— Luke Egan, Nick Wood (Richards' godson) and Matt Hoy—have followed the path he pioneered, none have captured the public imagination to the same extent.

In the lead-up to the 2000 Sydney Olympics, Mark Richards was handed one of sport's greatest honours: he was chosen to carry the Olympic torch on the final leg of its trip into the city. It was, he said, one of the most electrifying moments of his life.

parks

Careful planning over the decades has left Newcastle with an enviable array of pristine bush and wilderness areas within easy reach of the city centre. The region has eight National Parks and four State Recreation Areas within its boundaries, including Glenrock State Recreation Reserve at Burwood Beach, south of Merewether and the recently proclaimed Stockton Bight National Park.

Newcastle City Council's Blackbutt Reserve—a family favourite for generations—and the vast expanse of forest at Mount Sugarloaf, west of the city, are among the city's most popular bush attractions.

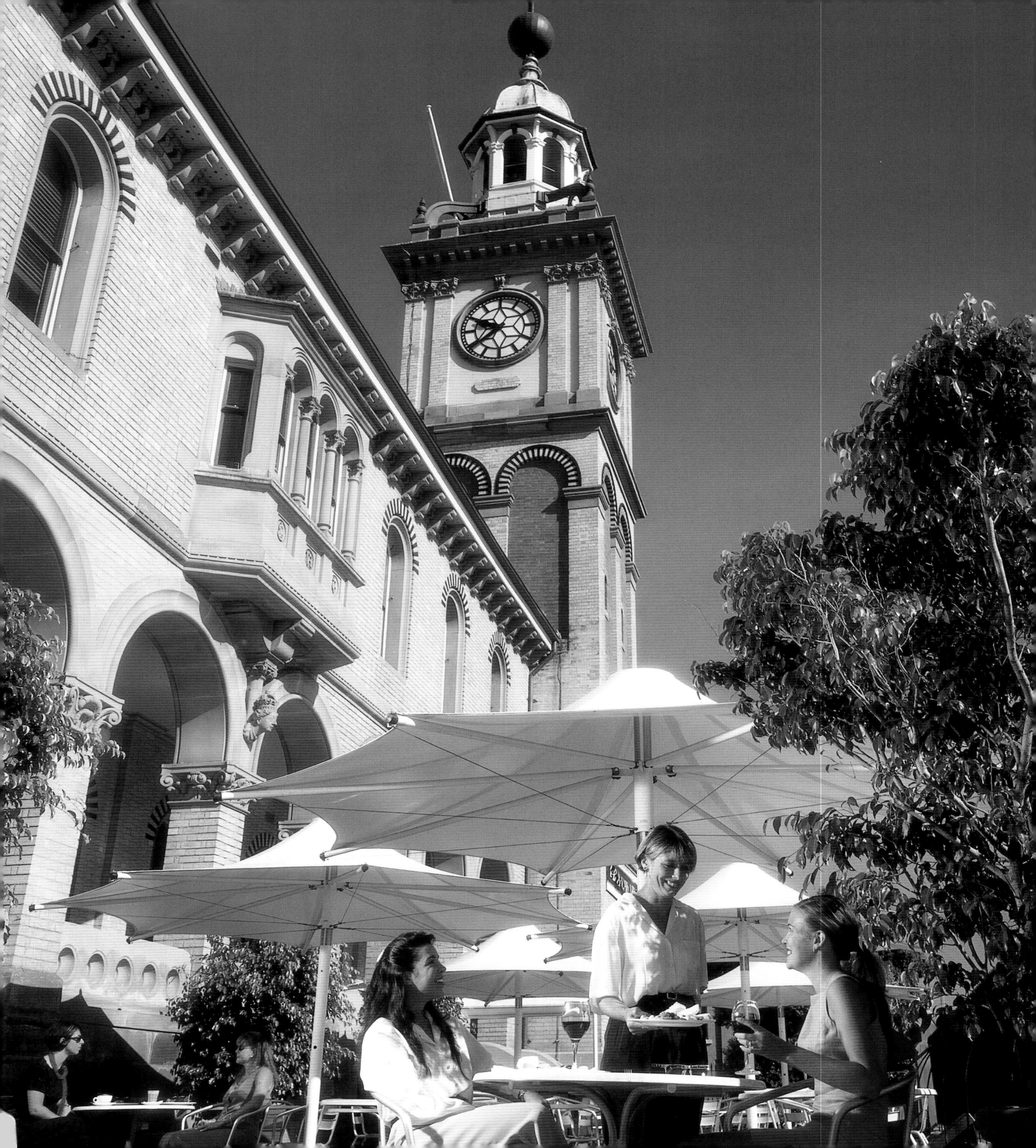

Like many post-industrial cities around the world, Newcastle has pinned much hope on tourism as a replacement job creator. The mainstay of its tourism is focused on domestic visitors, and its close proximity to Sydney make it a day-tripper's delight.

In packaging the area for visitors, tourism bodies have identified four areas within easy reach of Newcastle. From Pokolbin's world famous vineyards, to Port Stephens, Forster–Tuncurry and the Wallis Lakes to the north and Lake Macquarie to the south, Newcastle is surrounded by a range of single-day and overnight destinations.

The Barrington Tops and Watagan forests provide endless kilometres of walking trails through some of Australia's most stunning mountain scenery.

Maitland and its surrounding villages, especially Morpeth, are heritage treasure troves, featuring hundreds of heritage buildings, from stone mansions to the vernacular weatherboard workers' cottages that have survived from the first decades of the 19th century.

Port Stephens has an international reputation as a pleasure playground with a deep, safe waterway more than twice the size of Sydney Harbour. It has long been one of the globe's great game fishing grounds. Nelson Bay, the port's main commercial centre, is a thriving town of marinas, resorts and apartments. 'The Bay', as it's often known, has become a very popular holiday and weekend destination for Sydney residents. The rows of old fishing shacks along the eastern side of Port Stephens have almost all gone, now replaced with modern multi-storey homes with million-dollar price tags.

With 110 square kilometres of waterways and 175 kilometres of shoreline, Lake Macquarie is Australia's biggest coastal lake. Its sheer size divides communities on either side into separate areas, known popularly as East Lakes and West Lakes. Rapid population growth in the past 20 to 30 years has seen Lake Macquarie's population outstrip Newcastle's, with Charlestown growing into a business centre to complement Newcastle's established CBD.

Lake Macquarie boasts a youthful population with about 60 per cent under 40. Water is an integral part of the area's lifestyle; amateur and professional fishing, yachting, windsurfing, skiing and surfing are popular pursuits. The thousands of craft moored at the various marinas and yacht clubs dotted around the lake attest to this love of the water.

The old holiday villages spread along the shoreline are growing steadily under sustainable planning guidelines, and there is a mixture of weekend and permanent residents. Developments, such as the Raffertys Resort at Cams Wharf, are ushering in a new era of waterfront, resort-style holiday accommodation.

Newcastle plays an important role as the main medical centre for regional NSW—from the Central Coast to the Queensland border—with a modern growing set of hospital facilities based at the John Hunter Hospital.

The NSW government recently announced a $250 million overhaul of the Hunter Health system with upgrades to John Hunter, Belmont and the Mater Hospitals.

After a comprehensive year-long public consultation program, Hunter Health has announced plans to close Royal Newcastle Hospital opposite Newcastle Beach. The Royal is a Newcastle landmark, but in recent years the focus of health care has shifted squarely to the John Hunter.

One of the oldest sections of the hospital has already been sold and developers are proceeding with plans to recycle one historic building into luxury apartments with a residential tower planned for the beachfront side of the block.

The Royal is a key Newcastle development site and its future use is limited only by imagination.

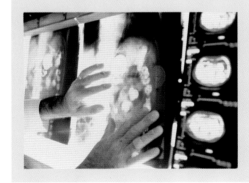

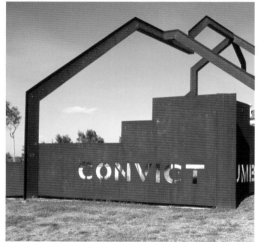

Newcastle has gained a strong reputation for its home grown talent, which is supported by a wealth of cultural events and venues. The Civic Theatre is one of Australia's great historic theatres and plays hosts to a range of local, national and international productions each year. The Shoot Out Film Festival, National Maritime Festival, National Young Writers Festival and Christ Church Cathedral Festival, are just a few of the happenings that attract national interest.

There are a number of indigenous performing arts and dance companies such as the Ngore-Rah Indigenous Performance Group and the Newcastle High School Aboriginal Dance Group, both of which produce works that express the views and stories of the indigenous community.

The Newcastle Regional Museum collects and displays historic objects representing the people, activities and places of the Hunter Region—a great place to learn more about the cultural heart and soul of the area. There are also a number of commercial galleries to satisfy art enthusiasts.

Another very important contributor to the region is the Newcastle Region Art Gallery (NRAG), home to some 3,000 works of art, offering a comprehensive view of Australian art from colonial times. John Glover, Arthur Sheeton, Margaret Preston, William Pobbel and Arthur Boyd are just a few of the artists represented. The NRAG 's regional significance was confirmed with a $600,000 sponsorship agreement with Channel Ten.

Newcastle Knights fans at Marathon Stadium.

football

For sports fans, the most exciting thing about Newcastle is its all-conquering rugby league team, the Newcastle Knights. The team has given the city the sort of positive national exposure it could once only dream about. In fact, for many sports-obsessed Australians, the first thing that springs to mind when you mention Newcastle is the rugby league team.

The Knights have done their city proud. The team joined the ranks of sporting immortals when as underdogs they won the 1997 Grand Final from favourites Manly with just eight seconds on the clock. It was the stuff of legend. The following week 100,000 people— 20 per cent of the Hunter's population—

crammed into the centre of Newcastle to pay homage to the humble, home-grown team.

The Newcastle Herald's sports editor, Kevin Cranson, captured the moment best when he wrote: 'Do not believe that this was just a football game; this was a defining moment in our town's history ...Yesterday we stormed the city and gave the rugby league team widely regarded as the best in the world a start and a beating.

'Then we turned around, and with the cry of "Newcastle" echoing behind us, we headed home. Home to a town of winners. Home to a place that no longer feels the need to apologise for itself or make excuses; to a place that has

come out of another's shadow and basks in its own bright light; home to a place that can match it with anyone.

'So believe that this was not just about football, for just as tragedy can unite a community, so too can triumph.'

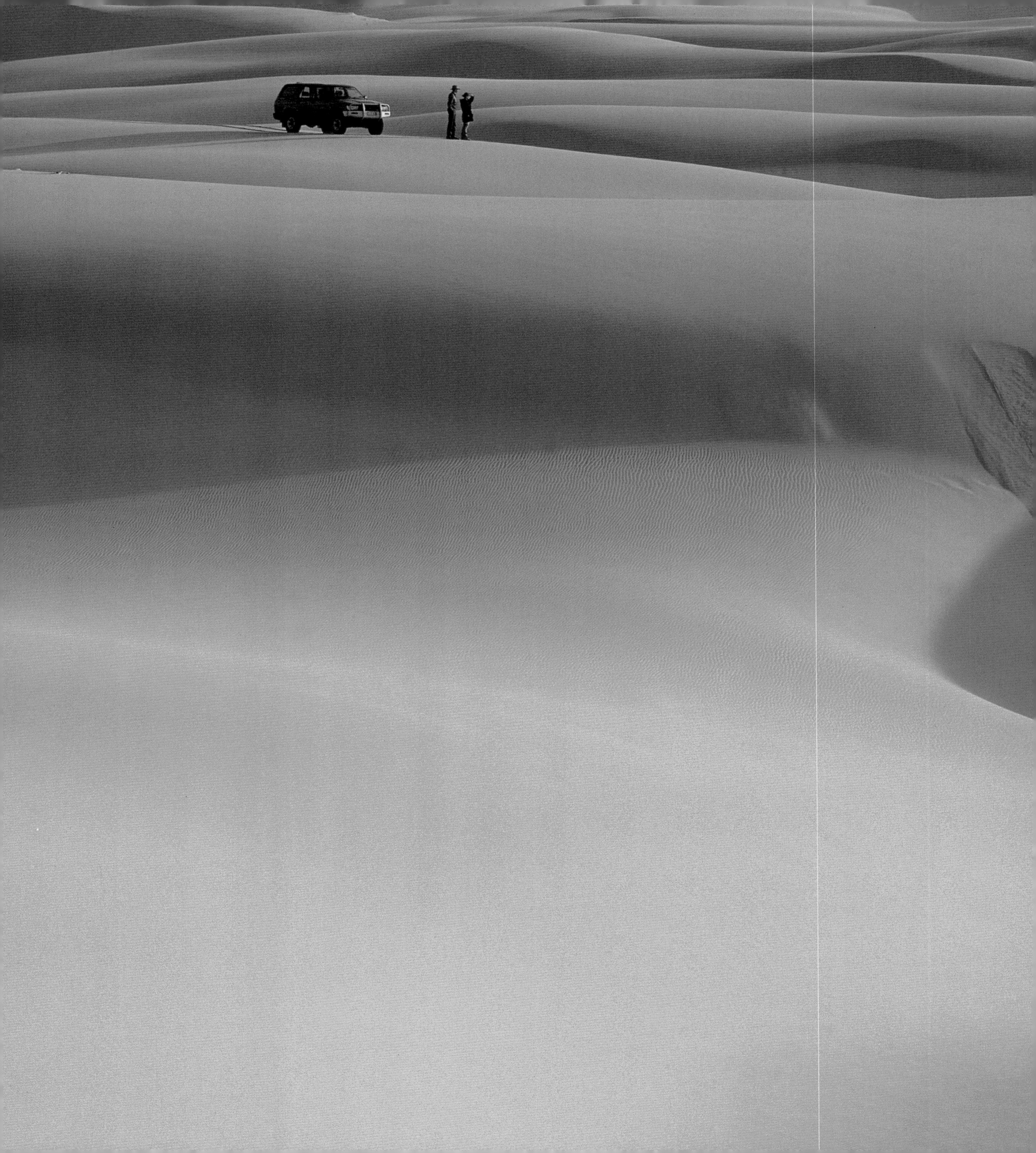

Careful planning over the decades has left Newcastle with an enviable array of pristine bush and wilderness areas within easy reach of the city centre.

Sand dunes at Stockton Bight, recently proclaimed a national park.

PAUL FOLEY'S
LIGHTMOODS PTY LTD

'As a professional photographer I'm paid to create imagery that helps convey a story about a person, business or locality. This pictorial story-telling in Newcastle and the Hunter is blessed by the diversity and beauty of the landscape and the enterprise of the people.'

—Paul Foley, Director, Paul Foley's Lightmoods Pty Ltd

Memorable Images

Readers of this book will react in one of two ways to the fine images of Newcastle and the Hunter—many the work of leading photographer Paul Foley, director of Paul Foley's Lightmoods Pty Ltd.

If the reader is a local, or knows the city and region well, many of the images will stir memories of good times, and reinforce the powerful bond with this city by the sea. If the reader is unfamiliar with Newcastle and its hinterland, the images may seem too good to be true, because they are often far removed from their perceptions.

Paul Foley has seen this reaction many times. 'If people haven't been here they have no idea how beautiful, diverse and inspiring the Hunter can be.'

Widely respected for his corporate, tourism and people photography, Paul has spent many hours at dawn and dusk, capturing the elusive moment that generates a memorable image, one that triggers an immediate emotional response in the viewer.

Paul and his cameras have travelled throughout the Hunter region and to many parts of the globe, but it is in the stretch of coastline from Merewether to Nobbys where he has created the signature pictures which demonstrate his dedication to this never-ending quest for perfection.

Many of those images now grace the walls of art lovers around the world, and are accessible through the Lightmoods Web-based stock image library. Paul Foley believes their universal appeal is a response to the complexities of modern life. 'They convey a sense of peace and space—even isolation—that is missing from our day-to-day lives.'

Paul Foley believes this opportunity to enjoy solitary moments is a key factor in the appeal of Newcastle and the Hunter as a place to live, work and raise a family. 'You can be working in the middle of the city and take a walk along the beach at lunchtime, with just the wind and waves for company. You don't have to battle the traffic and the madness of commuting and the people are welcoming.'

While his images deal with nature and the elements, and familiar icons of the local landscape, Paul Foley also enjoys photographing the human form and face. 'I require as much commitment from my subjects as they do from me. It's a challenge for both of us but my aim is to create a unique and lasting visual statement about the individual.'

While Paul uses the latest technology, creating scans and prints of the highest standards, he believes that the raw material, the memorable image, is what really counts. 'And for me there's no better place to capture those images than right here in the Hunter.'

See page 182 contact details >

NEWCASTLE : BUSINESS

'Horizons Golf Resort offers a unique experience. One of Australia's best golf courses, bushland setting with lots of native wildlife, the finest food and wine, facilities for all kinds of business functions, the warmest of welcomes, and a team that aims to please.'

—Antonio Gelonesi, Chief Executive Officer, Horizons Golf Resort

HORIZONS GOLF RESORT

Welcoming Horizons

For a taste of the best of the Hunter region lifestyle, Horizons Golf Resort has become a premier destination for locals and visitors alike. For those who enjoy a golfing challenge, the Horizon's championship course offers a test for players of all standards, from social golfers to skilled amateurs. Surrounded by natural bushland with abundant native wildlife, the par 72 layout designed by Graham Marsh and Ross Watson has been rated the state's top resort course since 1994, and among the top 10 in Australia.

If some practice is in order before taking on the rolling fairways, the driving range surrounded by wetlands is the ideal place to prepare the swing, and the spirit. While golf plays a significant role in business around the world, with many a deal clinched between tee and green, Horizons also offers first-class meeting and conference facilities.

After golf, visitors can enjoy the best in food and Hunter wine in the fine-dining restaurant, cafes or function rooms, relax in stylish condominiums or explore the waterways and wildlife of Port Stephens.

Just 25 minutes drive from Newcastle Airport and 45 minutes from the city, Horizons Golf Resort is a memorable experience, for business and pleasure.

See page 176 for contact details >

NEWCASTLE ENTERTAINMENT CENTRE/ CIVIC THEATRE NEWCASTLE

Newcastle's elegant Civic Theatre and multi-purpose Entertainment Centre host the best of Australian and international artists and shows. With excellent transport links servicing a catchment area that exceeds one million potential patrons, the venues make a significant contribution to the lifestyle and economy of Newcastle through a wide range of entertainment.

See page 179 for contact details >

NEWCASTLE : BUSINESS

'The *Newcastle Herald*'s aim is to produce a "one-stop" newspaper. We believe we cover major national and international events as well as any metropolitan paper, while our philosophy is to view those events through the eyes of firstly, Hunter Valley people, and secondly, regional and rural Australians. We believe we have the right mix— and our circulation and readership figures reflect that success.'

—Alan Oakley, Editor-in-Chief, Newcastle Newspapers

NEWCASTLE NEWSPAPERS PTY LTD

From humble beginnings more than 140 years ago, the *Newcastle Herald* and its parent company Newcastle Newspapers have grown to become one of the great regional Australian success stories.

Owned since 1977 by John Fairfax Holdings, publishers of the *Sydney Morning Herald* and the *Age*, Newcastle Newspapers employs more than 300 people and pumps more than $20 million a year into the Hunter economy.

The *Herald*'s historic offices were recently rebuilt and the presses shifted to a state-of-the-art facility at Beresfield, near the F3 west of Newcastle, at a total cost of more than $27.5 million.

The *Herald* is published six days a week, while the Hunter's free weekly paper, the *Post*, comes out on Wednesdays. The *Herald* went from broadsheet to tabloid in July 1998, and its circulation has skyrocketed by 16% in the first two years, making it Australia's fastest growing regional daily.

Both papers are an integral part of the Hunter community. The *Herald*'s reporting and commentary leads public debate in the region, and its coverage of local issues, from business and politics through to sport and entertainment, is second to none.

Newcastle Newspapers sponsors and supports a broad range of community interests and sporting events, and its school newspaper program gives school children practical experience in the media.

Advertising is a crucial part of the newspaper world, and the *Herald* and the *Post* classifieds are the region's instant guide to the real estate, motor and jobs markets. Both papers boast full-colour pages, giving display advertisers a winning edge.

See page 180 for contact details >

'Saddingtons has achieved its success in building products by capitalising on the strength of Newcastle and the opportunities the region provides. Change is inevitable and desirable. Through Newcastle's many years of continual change, Saddingtons has anchored its growth and reputation as a major contributor to the development of the area.'

—Bill and David Saddington, P W Saddington Pty Ltd

P W SADDINGTON PTY LTD

Building the Business

P W Saddington & Sons Pty Ltd was established in 1921 by Percy Saddington who sold local and imported grocery lines to wholesale and retail outlets. As Newcastle grew, the product lines expanded and the business sold a more diverse range of products, including building supplies.

In the early years after World War II, Percy and his son Dudley managed the business and the major focus turned toward the building industry. From this time Saddingtons continually expanded its range of specialised building supplies, to supply innovative products that advanced conventional building methods while offering exceptional service.

Today the company has three major building supply depots at Broadmeadow, Boolaroo and Rutherford. From these strategic locations a transport fleet of thirty vehicles makes deliveries to all building sites, domestic and commercial, in Newcastle, Lake Macquarie, the Hunter Valley and the Central Coast.

The scope of the Saddingtons Group of companies has expanded to include building supplies, building construction, hospitality and tourism. The staff of over 130 is managed by the third generation of the family, Bill and David Saddington.

See page 183 for contact details >

NEWCASTLE : BUSINESS

'Scratchleys is a showcase for all that this region aspires to be. Sustainable. Environmentally responsible. Great location and lifestyle. More and more businesses like ours are thinking not just of themselves, but of the big picture, of the contribution we can make to the future of Newcastle for our children.'

—Neil Slater, Proprietor and Restaurateur, Scratchleys Restaurant

SCRATCHLEYS RESTAURANT

Taking Time Out

In great cities around the world restaurants are a reflection of the character of their location, of the economy, the lifestyle, the culture and the history. Asked to nominate a restaurant, which typifies Newcastle and the Hunter, many Novocastrians would be quick to name Scratchleys.

Like much of the history and economic strength of the city, Scratchleys takes pride of place on Newcastle harbour. The original eatery was opened in a converted ferry terminal and soon became widely known for its fresh seafood and spectacular location.

When BHP announced the closure of its Newcastle Steelworks, owners Neil and Donna Slater wanted to help create a new image for the city as a premier tourist destination. Slater also wanted to showcase the region's environmental and sustainability credentials.

Just like the city, Scratchleys was reborn. A striking testament to its innovative, environmental architecture, the restaurant, bar and function centre has the continuous ebb and flow of maritime activity lapping at its doorstep.

The finest Hunter produce, wines and seafood, are also on show. Scratchleys is the first choice for proud locals to show off all the best the Hunter has to offer to admiring friends and visitors from around the world.

See page 185 for contact details >

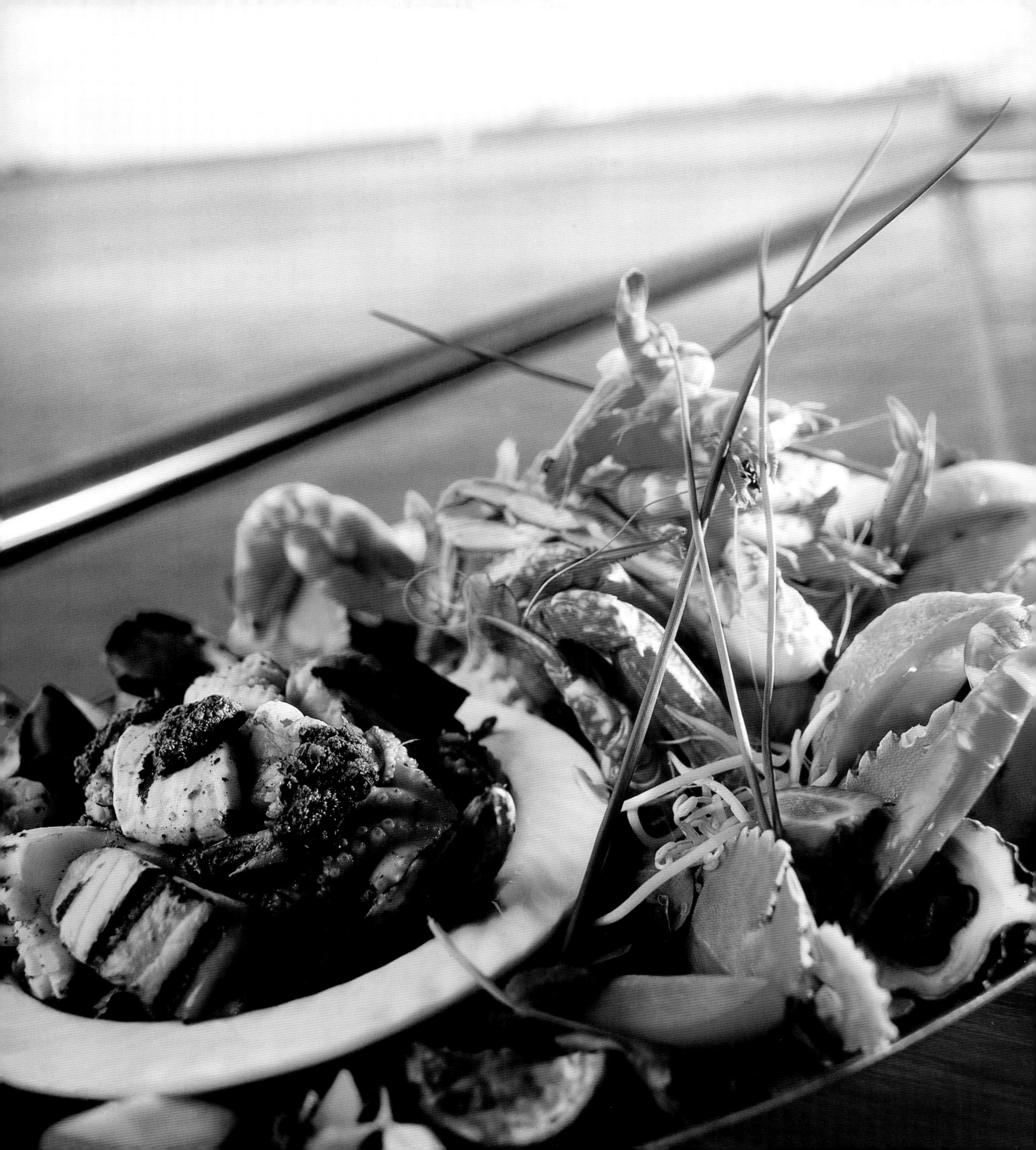

DIRECTORY OF PARTICIPANTS

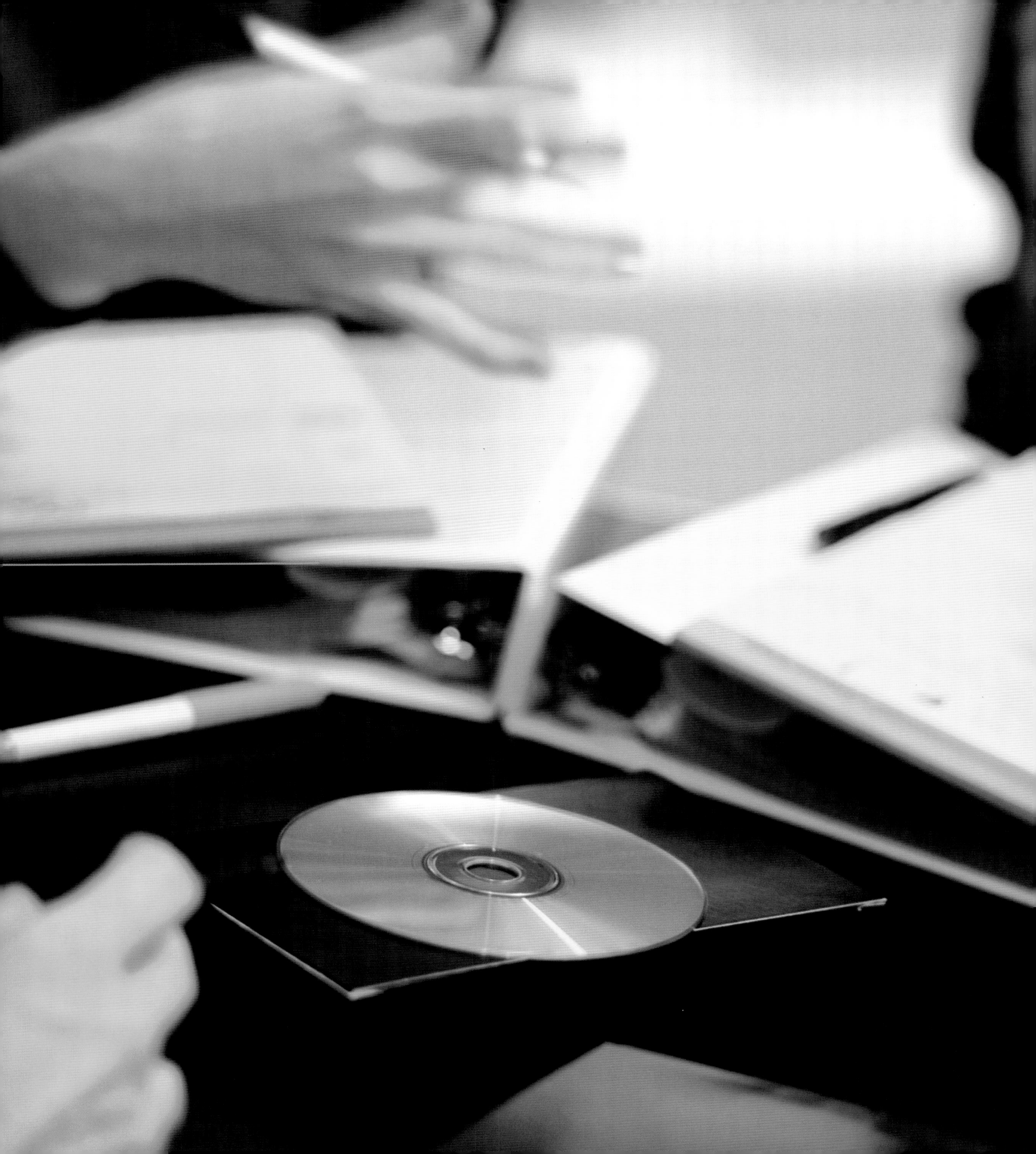

< See page 88 for business profile

Affordable Superiority

A Transfield – Thales company

In 1994, ADI and the Hunter 'teamed up' to win the Royal Australian Navy's Huon Class minehunter project. The Hunter enthusiastically supported ADI's bid and its goodwill toward ADI has never wavered. The highly successful project has duly rewarded the Hunter with local businesses winning contracts worth $300 million and providing 550 peak time jobs at ADI's Carrington site.

ADI Limited

Level 2, Building 51

Garden Island NSW 2011

Phone: (02) 9562 2552

Fax: (02) 9562 2387

Jean-Georges Malcor

Managing Director

www.adi-limited.com

< See page 132 for business profile

'AOK Health is an innovative exporter of products and services designed and tested in the Hunter. We provide continuing education programs for professional and corporate clients across Australia. Our teaching and service staff hold qualifications in a range of rehabilitation and sports sciences.'

—*Bradley Wilson, Managing Director, AOK Health Pty Ltd*

AOK Health Pty Ltd

31–33 Denison Street

Newcastle NSW 2302

Phone: (02) 4969 1101

Fax: (02) 4929 1151

Email: info@aokhealth.com.au

Bradley Wilson

Managing Director

www.aokhealth.com.au

< See pages 22–27 for business profile

The City of
Newcastle

'We tell visitors to Newcastle "Be prepared to be surprised" because it happens all the time. People come here with perceptions that are soon blown away by our quality of life, our environment and the opportunities the city offers.'

—Councillor John S Tate, Lord Mayor, The City of Newcastle

Newcastle City Council
282 King Street
Newcastle NSW 2300

PO Box 489
Newcastle NSW 2300

Phone: (02) 4974 2000
Fax: (02) 4974 2222
Email: mail@ncc.nsw.gov.au

Councillor John S Tate
Lord Mayor

Janet Dore
General Manager

www.ncc.nsw.gov.au

< See page 147 for business profile

'Experience on a wide variety of major projects in the Hunter region has given Daracon the skills and capability to keep on winning major contracts. The company's commitment to quality, safety and the environment ensures the company is a leader in the industry.'

—David Mingay, Managing Director, Daracon Group

Daracon Engineering Pty Ltd
17 James Street
Wallsend NSW 2287

Phone: (02) 4951 8555
Fax: (02) 4951 1070
Email: dgroup@daracon.com.au

David Mingay
Managing Director

www.daracon.com.au

< See page 133 for business profile

< See pages 104–105 for business profile

'The Delta EMD plant at Newcastle is a world-class operation in terms of performance, quality and the environment. All activities are directed towards one single aim—meeting the needs of our customers—hence our strong commitment to research partnerships with major battery manufacturers.'

—*Evan van Zyl, Chairman and Managing Director*
Delta EMD Australia Pty Limited

Delta EMD Australia Pty Limited
Steel River Industrial Estate, McIntosh Drive
Mayfield West NSW 2304

Phone: (02) 4941 1500
Fax: (02) 4941 1555
Email: scanlon.john.rj@deltaemd.com.au

Evan W van Zyl
Chairman and Managing Director

Richard J Scanlon
Finance Director

'EnergyAustralia is undertaking its biggest capital works program for decades to ensure Newcastle has first-class electricity infrastructure to support the region's growth. This will be a fundamental plank in ensuring the Hunter region can reach its potential and develop even further as a leading business and tourism centre.'

—*Paul A Broad, Managing Director, EnergyAustralia*

EnergyAustralia
570 George Street
Sydney NSW 2000

Phone: 13 15 25
Fax: (02) 9269 2830

Paul A Broad
Managing Director

www.energy.com.au

< See page 62

'GrainCorp delivers storage and logistics solutions for bulk grain export at its Newcastle terminal. Through dedication to our customers, by diversifying core business activities and embracing change, we will continue our strong contribution to Newcastle—well into the new century.'

—*John Sneddon, GrainCorp Newcastle Terminal Manager*

GrainCorp Operations Ltd

Level 10, 51 Druitt Street

Sydney NSW 2000

Phone: +61 2 9325 9100

Fax: +61 2 9325 9180

Email: inquiries@graincorp.com.au

Ron Greentree

Chairman

Tom Keene

Managing Director

www.graincorp.com.au

< See page 148 for business profile

'There are terrific development opportunities at Honeysuckle, a major catalyst for the re-imaging and revitalisation of inner Newcastle. Over 20 years the Honeysuckle redevelopment project will inject dollars into the regional economy, create new jobs and attract more new residents to the inner city.'

—*David Le Marchant, Chairman, Honeysuckle Development Corporation*

Honeysuckle Development Corporation

Level 2, 251 Wharf Road

Newcastle NSW 2300

Phone: (02) 4927 3800

Fax: (02) 4929 1927

Email: honeysuckle@duap.nsw.gov.au

David Le Marchant

Chairman

Angus Dawson

General Manager

www.honeysuckledc.com.au

< See page 164 for business profile

< See page 134 for business profile

'Horizons Golf Resort offers a unique experience. One of Australia's best golf courses, bushland setting with lots of native wildlife, the finest food and wine, facilities for all kinds of business functions, the warmest of welcomes, and a team that aims to please.'

—Antonio Gelonesi, Chief Executive Officer, Horizons Golf Resort

'The future of education and training lies in our ability to share our strengths and broaden the opportunities for all.'

—Dr Gaye Hart, Director, Hunter Institute of Technology
and Professor Roger Holmes, Vice Chancellor & President,
The University of Newcastle

Horizons Golf Resort

5 Horizons Drive

Salamander Bay NSW 2317

Phone: (02) 4982 0502

Fax: (02) 4982 0150

Email: enquiries@horizonsgolfresort.com.au

Antonio Gelonesi

Chief Executive Officer

Hunter Institute of Technology—TAFE NSW

Locked Bag 45

Hunter Region Mail Centre NSW 2310

Phone: +61 2 4923 7222

Dr Gaye Hart

Institute Director

The University of Newcastle, Australia

The Chancellary, University Drive

Callaghan NSW 2308

Phone: +61 2 4921 5000

Professor Roger Holmes

Vice Chancellor & President

www.horizons.com.au

www.hunter.tafensw.edu.au
www.newcastle.edu.au

< See page 63 for business profile

< See page 89 for business profile

KOPPERS

'Take away the barriers and companies can fulfil their real potential. Ipera can deliver much more telecommunications capacity to business than traditional solutions at a fraction of the cost. That benefit can then be leveraged to provide innovative solutions to business problems ... and even more competitive advantage!'

—*Chris Deere, Managing Director, Ipera Network Computing Pty Ltd*

Ipera Network Computing Pty Ltd

9 Denison Street

Newcastle West NSW 2302

Phone: (02) 4940 6666

Fax: (02) 4940 6633

Email: info@ipera.com.au

Chris Deere

Managing Director

Armand Hoitink

Business Operations Manager

'Koppers Coal Tar Products is the legacy of our history of local investment in the Hunter region. We are a part of a thriving industrial community in Newcastle and our innovative use of resources is welcomed by other key employers such as aluminium smelters in the Lower Hunter.'

—*Ernie Bryon, Managing Director, Koppers Coal Tar Products Pty Ltd*

Koppers Coal Tar Products Pty Ltd

Head office

15 Blue Street

North Sydney NSW 2060

Phone: (02) 9954 5411

Plant Address

Woodstock Street

Mayfield NSW 2304

Phone: (02) 4968 7320

Ernie Bryon

Managing Director

www.ipera.com.au

< See pages 80–81 for business profile

< See page 116–117 for business profile

'Although Marathon Tyres is now considering international opportunities, our commitment to the Hunter region remains as strong as ever. With strong partnerships, the right people and a passion to do the job right, Newcastle is a great place to start and build a successful business.'

—Mike Nesbitt, Chairman, Marathon Tyres Pty Ltd

Marathon Tyres Pty Ltd
10 Friesian Close
Sandgate NSW 2304

Phone: (02) 4960 2144
Fax: (02) 4968 8256
Email: reception@marathontyres.com.au

Michael Nesbitt
Chief Executive Officer

Gregory Nesbitt
Director

'Newcastle Airport prides itself on linking the Hunter to Australia and the rest of the world. It makes a substantial contribution to the regional economy by establishing client partnerships, identifying customer and market opportunities, making provisions which exceed customer expectations and actively promoting the Airport as the aviation gateway to this magnificent region.'

—Air Vice Marshal Richard J Bomball AO AFC (retired), Chairman, Newcastle Airport Limited

Newcastle Airport Limited
Private Bag 1
Williamtown NSW 2318

Phone: (02) 4965 1925
Fax: (02) 4965 1927
Email: admin@newcastleairport.com.au

Air Vice Marshal Richard J Bomball AO, AFC (retired)
Chairman

www.marathontyres.com.au

www.newcastleairport.com.au

< See page 165

< See page 130–131 for business profile

Newcastle Entertainment Centre
Showground, Broadmeadow NSW

CIVIC THEATRE
NEWCASTLE
· AUSTRALIA'S PREMIER REGIONAL THEATRE

HUNTER HEALTH
Improving Health in the Hunter

Hunter Urban Division
of General Practice

HMRI
hunter medical research institute

Newcastle's elegant Civic Theatre and multi-purpose Entertainment Centre host the best of Australian and international artists and shows. With excellent transport links servicing a catchment area that exceeds one million potential patrons, the venues make a significant contribution to the lifestyle and economy of Newcastle through a wide range of entertainment.

Newcastle Entertainment Centre
Brown Road
Broadmeadow NSW 2292

Phone: (02) 4921 2100
Fax: (02) 4921 2199
Email: admin@nentcent.com.au

Civic Theatre Newcastle
375 Hunter Street
Newcastle NSW 2300

Phone: (02) 4929 1561
Fax: (02) 4926 5460
Email: admin@civictheatrenewcastle.com.au

Newcastle Health Services

Hunter Health
Lookout Road
New Lambton Heights NSW 2305
Phone: (02) 4921 4960
Professor Katherine McGrath
Chief Executive Officer

Hunter Urban Division of General Practice
Level 3, 123 King Street
Newcastle NSW 2300
Phone: (02) 4925 2259
Dr Arn Sprogis
Executive Director

Hunter Medical Research Institute
Locked Bag 1
New Lambton NSW 2305
Phone: (02) 4921 4841
Professor John Rostas
Executive Director

www.nentcent.com.au
www.civictheatrenewcastle.com.au

www.hunter.health.nsw.gov.au
www.hudgp.org.au
www.hmri.net.au

< See page 166 for business profile

< See pages 40–41 for business profile

NEWCASTLE HERALD

'The *Newcastle Herald*'s aim is to produce a "one-stop" newspaper. We believe we cover major national and international events as well as any metropolitan paper, while our philosophy is to view those events through the eyes of firstly, Hunter Valley people, and secondly, regional and rural Australians. We believe we have the right mix—and our circulation and readership figures reflect that success.'

—*Alan Oakley, Editor-in-Chief, Newcastle Newspapers*

Newcastle Newspapers Pty Ltd

28–30 Bolton Street

Newcastle NSW 2300

Phone: (02) 4979 5000

Fax: (02) 4979 5988 (editorial)

Fax: (02) 4979 5288 (advertising)

Email: ntlinfo@newcastle.fairfax.com.au

Brian Evans

General Manager

Alan Oakley

Editor-in-Chief

www.nnp.com.au

'The Newcastle Permanent is a large local mutual financial institution with our financial strength derived from the support of our strong regional community over many years. I am confident of a dynamic and bright future for our region and we look forward to playing a significant role in this future as the complete financial services provider.'

—*Howard Frith, Managing Director, Newcastle Permanent Building Society Limited*

Newcastle Permanent Building Society Limited

307 King Street

Newcastle NSW 2300

Phone: (02) 4926 1133

Fax: (02) 4929 4637

Email: marketing@newcastlepermanent.com.au

Howard Frith

Managing Director

Barrie Lewis

Chairman

www.newcastlepermanent.com.au

< See pages 118–119 for business profile

NEWCASTLE PORT CORPORATION

'The only certainty is change. As demands in world markets change, so do the needs of Hunter industries. It's the role of Newcastle Port Corporation to create business opportunities or respond to those industry needs, to ensure links between the region and world markets are efficient, effective and flexible.'

—Glen Oakley, Chief Executive Officer

Newcastle Port Corporation

Newcastle Port Corporation
Corner Scott & Newcomen Streets
Newcastle NSW 2300

Phone: (02) 4985 8222
Fax: (02) 4926 4596
Email: mail@newportcorp.com

Glen Oakley
Chief Executive Officer

Tim Ryan
Business Relations Manager

www.newportcorp.com

< See page 44 for business profile

nib
Health cover
for every*body*

'NIB Health Funds is an important part of the Hunter's social and economic fabric. We provide first-class health care for members, and support initiatives that make a contribution to improved health and lifestyle in the wider community. Above all, NIB's business growth from our Hunter headquarters is one of the region's true success stories.'

—Colin Rogers, Managing Director, NIB Health Funds Ltd

NIB Health Funds Ltd
384 Hunter Street
Newcastle NSW 2300

Phone: (02) 4921 2400
Fax: (02) 4926 2310
Email: nib@nib.com.au

Colin Rogers
Managing Director

John Moore
Chairman

www.nib.com.au

181

< *See page 90 for business profile*

< *See pages 162–163 for business profile*

onesteel

Paul Foley's
Lightmoods

'OneSteel has strong historical links with Newcastle. Our strong market position is driven by our assets, our technology, our people and the strength and support of the community in Newcastle.'

—*Geoff Plummer, President, Market Mills*

'As a professional photographer I'm paid to create imagery that helps convey a story about a person, business or locality. This pictorial story-telling in Newcastle and the Hunter is blessed by the diversity and beauty of the landscape and the enterprise of the people.'

—*Paul Foley, Director, Paul Foley's Lightmoods Pty Ltd*

OneSteel Limited

Level 23, 1 York Street

Sydney NSW 2000

GPO Box 536

Sydney NSW 2001

Ph: (02) 9239 6666

Fax: (02) 9251 3042

Dr Robert Every

Managing Director and CEO

Peter Smedley

Chairman

Paul Foley's Lightmoods Pty Ltd

PO Box 277

The Junction NSW 2291

Phone: (02) 4962 2140

Fax: (02) 4962 2404

Email: info@lightmoods.com.au

Paul Foley

Director

www.onesteel.com

www.lightmoods.com.au

< See page 91 for business profile

< See page 167 for business profile

'Along with determination to achieve a high level of coal loading efficiency, PWCS combines dedication to quality and commitment to the environment and the safety of its employees, with recognition of its role in the Hunter community. PWCS will maintain this dedication and commitment as demand for Hunter coal continues to grow.'

—David Brewer, General Manager, Port Waratah Coal Services Ltd

Port Waratah Coal Services Ltd
PO Box 57
Carrington NSW 2294

Phone: (02) 4907 2000
Fax: (02) 4907 3000

Professor Eileen Doyle
Chairman

David Brewer
General Manager

'Saddingtons has achieved its success in building products by capitalising on the strength of Newcastle and the opportunities the region provides. Change is inevitable and desirable. Through Newcastle's many years of continual change, Saddingtons has anchored its growth and reputation as a major contributor to the development of the area.'

—Bill and David Saddington, PW Saddington Pty Ltd

P W Saddington Pty Ltd
75–81 Lambton Road
Broadmeadow NSW 2292

Phone: (02) 4969 6422
Fax: (02) 4940 8762
Email: saddingtons@bigpond.com

William Saddington
Managing Director

David Saddington
Director

www.pwcs.com.au **www.saddingtons.com.au**

183

< See pages 82–83 for business profile

Robtec Control Solutions Pty Ltd

17 Callistemon Close

Warabrook NSW 2304

Phone: (02) 4968 2888

Robert Nichols

Chief Executive Officer

Michael Smallcombe

Marketing Manager

Control Synergy Pty Ltd

PO Box 303

Hunter Region Mail Centre NSW 2310

Phone: (02) 4908 2222

Robert Nichols

Chief Executive Officer

David Croxford

National Marketing Manager

www.robtec.com.au
www.controlsynergy.com.au

< See pages 84–85 for business profile

'For a major international company like Sandvik, a strong presence in the Hunter is important. The strength of the mining and metals industries in the region alone means Sandvik products and services are in high demand. The quality of those products and services makes Hunter industries more efficient and competitive.'

—David Macdonald, Sandvik Australia Pty Ltd

Sandvik Australia Pty Ltd

Cnr Warren and Percival Roads

Smithfield NSW 2164

Phone: (02) 9828 0500

Fax: (02) 9828 0505

Email: john.armitage@sandvik.com

J K Ellis

Chairman

John Armitage

Managing Director

www.sandvik.com

< See page 168 for business profile

'Scratchleys is a showcase for all that this region aspires to be. Sustainable. Environmentally responsible. Great location and lifestyle. More and more businesses like ours are thinking not just of themselves, but of the big picture, of the contribution we can make to the future of Newcastle for our children.'

—Neil Slater, Proprietor and Restaurateur, Scratchleys Restaurant

Scratchleys Restaurant

200 Wharf Road

Newcastle NSW 2300

Phone: (02) 4929 1111

Fax: (02) 4929 6988

Neil Slater

Proprietor and Restaurateur

www.scratchleys.com.au

< See page 45 for business profile

'Sharp Electronics Office National, a local company of 30 years, supplying Business Equipment Solutions, believes the Hunter region certainly is a great "Centre for Business". Newcastle is a diversified business centre, has always embraced changes in new technology, and adapts well to an ever-changing market. Our growth and success stems from our ability to provide innovative solutions and excellent after sales service.'

—Ben Hickson, General Manager, Sharp Electronics Office National

Sharp Electronics Office National

Head Office: 89–93 Lambton Road

Broadmeadow NSW 2292

Phone: (02) 4962 1313

Fax: (02) 4962 1551

Email: sharp@sharpnew.com.au

John Duncan

Managing Director

Ben Hickson

General Manager

www.sharpnew.com.au

< See page 46 for business profile

Your Partners for the Future

'Sparke Helmore is an energetic, innovative and progressive law firm with a clear and focused vision for the future. Founded in Newcastle and through strategic placement of offices in Newcastle, Muswellbrook, Sydney, Melbourne, Canberra, Brisbane and Adelaide, the firm meets the high standards and volumes of work demanded by the government, business and insurance sectors in the major economic centres of Australia.'

—Paul Anicich, Partner, Sparke Helmore Solicitors

Sparke Helmore Solicitors

Levels 1–5, 21 Bolton Sreet

Newcastle NSW 2300

Phone: (02) 4924 7200

Fax: (02) 4924 7299

Email: helmore@sparke.com.au

www.sparke.com.au

< See page 120 for business profile

'The values of hard work and enterprise which underpinned Albert Toll's world in 1888 are ingrained in the company today. We have a strong interest in the Hunter, and not just because of its status as a key regional port in Australia. Part of having an eye on the future is remembering our past. The Hunter is a big part of both.'

—Steven Ford, General Manager

Toll Logistics, Ports and Resources Division

Toll Logistics

19 Nelson Road

Cardiff NSW 2285

Phone: (02) 4902 5300

Fax: (02) 4956 5083

Email: tollports@toll.com.au

Steven Ford

General Manager, Ports and Resources Division

www.tollports.com.au

< See page 92 for business profile

'Tomago Aluminium is proud of its role as a major employer, exporter and revenue earner for the Hunter. We are continually looking at ways to increase the efficiency of our operations to competitively position the plant globally, attract further investment to the Hunter and secure the long-term future of the industry in this region.'

—Doug Parrish, Plant Manager

Tomago Aluminium Company Pty Limited

Tomago Aluminium Company Pty Limited
Tomago Road
Tomago NSW 2322

Phone: (02) 4966 9669
Fax: (02) 4866 9711

Doug Parrish
Plant Manager

www.tomago.com.au

< See page 121 for business profile

UNITED GONINAN

'As part of United Group Limited, Goninan continues its proud history now as United Goninan. With 14 operations throughout Australia and South-East Asia and over 1,200 employees, United Goninan is committed to the growth and development of its business, employees and the Hunter region.'

—Allan Smith, Managing Director, United Goninan

United Goninan
Broadmeadow Road
Broadmeadow NSW 2292

Phone: (02) 4923 5000
Fax: (02) 4923 5001

Allan Smith
Managing Director

Mark Parkinson
Executive General Manager Finance & Administration

A United Group Limited Company

www.unitedgroup.com.au

< See pages 86–87 for business profile

VARLEY
EXCELLENCE SINCE 1886

'In critical sectors such as defence, we have to provide solutions that are absolutely right the first time around. There is no margin for error. And the quality has to be of the highest order, because the next test will be under battle conditions and lives will depend on our products.'

—Jeff Phillips, Chairman and Managing Director

Varley Holdings Pty Ltd

Varley Holdings Pty Ltd
21 School Drive
Tomago NSW 2322

Phone: (02) 4964 0400
Fax: (02) 4964 0499
Email: Sales@varleygroup.com

Jeff Phillips
Chairman and Managing Director

Jim Marshall
Operations Director

www.varleygroup.com

< See page 149 for business profile

STRONACH

'Since 1927, when William Stronach laid the foundations for the grand Civic Theatre, the Stronach name has been synonymous with building excellence, with a reputation for professionalism, trust and loyalty, reinvesting in the future of the region with an innovative approach to the entire development process, from design to financing of major projects.'

—Keith Stronach, Managing Director, W Stronach Pty Ltd

W Stronach Pty Ltd
3 Bradford Close
Kotara NSW 2289

Phone: (02) 4952 6777
Fax: (02) 4952 8187
Email: mail@stronach.com.au

Alan Taylor
Development Manager

Courtney Sharp
Manager Building Operations

www.stronach.com.au

< See pages 42–43 for business profile

'The key factor in the success of Websters Australia is quality assurance. We have taken that principle and followed it through every aspect of our operation, from training to recruitment, and all our field activities, including corporate and security protection, emergency and medical management and facilities management.'

—*Phillip Egge, Managing Director, Websters Australia Pty Ltd*

Websters Australia Pty Ltd

Head Office

419 Hunter Street

Newcastle NSW 2300

Phone: (02) 4929 5180

Fax: (02) 4926 5370

Email: phillip@websters-newcastle.com.au

Phillip Egge

Managing Director, Head Office Newcastle

Robert Epps

General Manager, Sydney Metropolitan Region

www.websters-newcastle.com.au

A Focus Publishing Book Project

Focus Publishing Pty Ltd

ABN 55 003 600 360

PO Box 518 Edgecliff NSW 2027

Phone: +61 2 9327 4777

Fax: +61 2 9362 3753

Email: focus@focus.com.au

Website: www.focus.com.au

Project Manager: Vic Hankins

Senior Editor: Kevin Pyle

Designer: Deidre Stein

Client Services: Mary Murabito, Kate Sanday

Production Manager: Timothy Ho

Chairman: Steven Rich AM

Publisher: Jaqui Lane

Managing Editor: Philippa Sandall

Associate Publisher: Gillian Fitzgerald

Corporate Communications: Gloria Nykl

For information on Focus Publishing visit **www.focus.com.au**

ISBN 1 875359 85 0

PICTURE CREDITS

Images used in the chapters of this book have been kindly supplied by Paul Foley's Lightmoods Pty Ltd (refer to the business profile on pages 162–163) with the exception of the following: ADI Limited, page 74 (right); BAE SYSTEMS, page 76; Hunter Economic Development Corporation (HEDC), pages 58 (bottom), 126, 127; Hunter Health, page 15 (bottom); Newcastle Port Corporation, pages 108–109, 112–113, 138–139; PhotoDisc Inc, pages 18, 53, 55 (left, middle), 68, 69, 71, 93, 128 (middle), 146,157 (bottom), 171, 190 (bottom).

ADI LIMITED
www.adi-limited.com

AOK Health Pty Ltd
www.aokhealth.com.au

Daracon Engineering Pty Ltd
www.daracon.com.au

Delta EMD Australia Pty Ltd
Email:
scanlon.john.rj@deltaemd.com.au

EnergyAustralia
www.energy.com.au

GrainCorp Operations Ltd
www.graincorp.com.au

Honeysuckle Development Corporation
www.honeysuckledc.com.au

Horizons Golf Resort
www.horizons.com.au

Hunter Institute of Technology—TAFE
NSW / The University of Newcastle
www.hunter.tafensw.edu.au
www.newcastle.edu.au

Ipera Network Computing Pty Ltd
www.ipera.com.au

Koppers Coal Tar Products Pty Ltd
Email: Info@koppers.com.au

Marathon Tyres
www.marathontyres.com.au

Newcastle Airport Limited
www.newcastleairport.com.au

Newcastle City Council
www.ncc.nsw.gov.au

Newcastle Entertainment Centre /
Civic Theatre Newcastle
www.nentcent.com.au
www.civictheatrenewcastle.com.au

Newcastle Health Services
www.hunter.health.nsw.gov.au
www.hudgp.org.au
www.hmri.net.au

Newcastle Newspapers Pty Ltd
www.nnp.com.au

Newcastle Permanent Building Society
Limited
www.newcastlepermanent.com.au

Newcastle Port Corporation
www.newportcorp.com

NIB Health Fund Ltd
www.nib.com.au

OneSteel Limited
www.onesteel.com

Paul Foley's Lightmoods Pty Ltd
www.lightmoods.com.au

Port Waratah Coal Services Ltd
www.pwcs.com.au

P W Saddington Pty Ltd
www.saddingtons.com.au

Robtec Control Solutions Pty Ltd /
Control Synergy Pty Ltd
www.robtec.com.au
www.controlsynergy.com.au

Sandvik Australia Pty Ltd
www.sandvik.com

Scratchleys Restaurant
www.scratchleys.com.au

Sharp Electronics Office National
www.sharpnew.com.au

Sparke Helmore Solicitors
www.sparke.com.au

Toll Logistics
www.tollports.com.au

Tomago Aluminium Company Pty Limited
www.tomago.com.au

United Goninan
www.unitedgroup.com.au

Varley Holdings Pty Ltd
www.varleygroup.com

W Stronach Pty Ltd
www.stronach.com.au

Websters Australia Pty Ltd
www.websters-newcastle.com.au

index

index

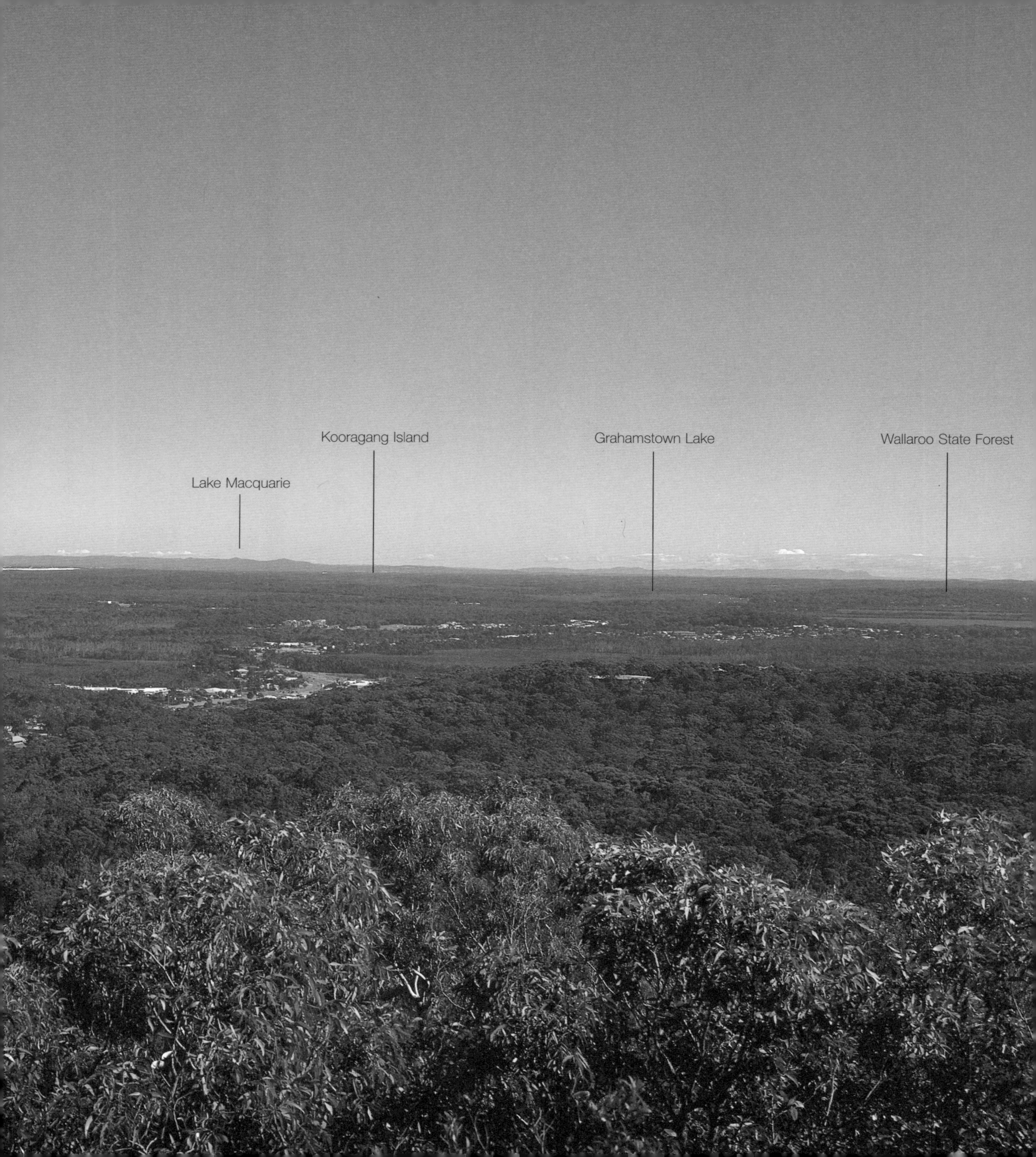
Lake Macquarie
Kooragang Island
Grahamstown Lake
Wallaroo State Forest